COOK TO
THRIVE

COOK TO THRIVE

Recipes to Fuel Body and Soul

NATALIE COUGHLIN

Clarkson Potter/Publishers
NEW YORK

Published in the United States by Clarkson Potter/Publishers, an imprint of the
Crown Publishing Group, a division of Penguin Random House LLC, New York.
crownpublishing.com
clarksonpotter.com

CLARKSON POTTER is a trademark and POTTER with colophon is a registered
trademark of Penguin Random House LLC.

Library of Congress Cataloging-in-Publication Data
Names: Coughlin, Natalie, author.
Title: Cook to thrive : recipes to fuel body and soul / Natalie Coughlin.
Description: First edition. | New York : Clarkson Potter/Publishers, [2019] |
    Includes index.
Identifiers: LCCN 2018016145 | ISBN 9781524762179 (hardcover) | ISBN
    9781524762186 (ebook)
Subjects: LCSH: Cooking (Natural foods) | Nutrition. | LCGFT: Cookbooks.
Classification: LCC TX741 .C69 2019 | DDC 641.3/02—dc23
LC record available at https://lccn.loc.gov/2018016145

ISBN 978-1-5247-6217-9
Ebook ISBN 978-1-5247-6218-6

Printed in China

Book and cover design by Sonia Persad
Photographs by Erin Kunkel

10 9 8 7 6 5 4 3 2 1

First Edition

For my mom

CONTENTS

INTRODUCTION

To most people, I'm known as an Olympian. As a competitor in the 2004, 2008, and 2012 Olympics, I earned three golds, four silvers, and five bronzes swimming for Team USA (no female American Olympian has won more medals). Many also know that I've had great success in swimming beyond the Olympics, having earned over sixty major international medals over my two-decade-long career.

Yet those of you who follow me on Facebook, Twitter, and Instagram know that besides swimming, my biggest passion is food. I love all aspects of it: cooking, transforming ingredients into something delicious both for my own enjoyment and for sharing with others; growing herbs, vegetables, and fruits in my backyard, where I also raise chickens; and, most important, eating! I've even cooked on NBC's *Today,* competed on Food Network's *Chopped,* and been a judge on Food Network's *Iron Chef America.* Food has always been a significant part of my life, so I'm thrilled to be able to share my favorite recipes, some handy kitchen tips, stories from my life and career, and my whole approach to cooking—since food makes a huge difference in my profession—in my first cookbook.

Having grown up swimming competitively, I learned early on that food is fuel and that to perform at the highest level of your sport, you need to consume the best-quality fuel. On the Olympic level, you find that athletes put this concept into practice in all sorts of ways. Some athletes count every macronutrient and put their stock in repeated meals of bland chicken breast, steamed broccoli, and brown rice, believing these Spartan foods to be what their body needs to compete at its best. Other athletes focus on the quantity of calories as their key to success, believing that since their caloric needs are so intense, it doesn't matter what they are consuming, as long as they're eating a lot. There are many ways to fuel a body, and finding what's best for me has long been a top priority.

But I also grew up in a family that valued food for reasons that have nothing to do with pure function. Cooking family recipes at home, eating together as often as possible, and always celebrating holidays and events with an abundance of homemade dishes have shaped my entire life. My mother did her best to ensure that our family ate together every night, somehow managing to whip up stir-fries or other from-scratch meals for us after long days of work. I'm grateful now for her commitment to feeding us so well—and grateful that I actually learned something about cooking in those years, in spite of my picky food habits! Holidays were a sight to behold, too, with my grandma always creating an incredibly generous spread for her family. Though my blue eyes and lighter skin don't show it, my mother's family is from the Philippines, and Filipino culture is all about delicious food. Grandma outdid herself with the number of homemade dishes—both Filipino and American—that she'd load onto the dining table. My mom and grandma showed their love for their families through feeding them, and as a result, I will always associate cooking and sharing food with love and caring.

So as I learned to hone my diet for the sake of my sport, I knew that I had to find my own path of optimal eating that balanced enjoyment with functionality. Many athletes approach their training with a strict "all or nothing" approach, but that never worked for me. There was no way I'd give up certain comfort foods—such as Grandma's Lumpia (page 128), a traditional Filipino fried snack that she makes in abundance for holidays—because even attempting to do so would throw me off any nutritional plan I was on. But my body can't handle the stress of training if I *only* eat lumpia (sorry, Grandma!).

I've cooked for myself during my entire swimming career, developing a diet that could sustain my body for the long term, through demanding training seasons and intense competitions. I focus on consuming nutrient-dense foods that will give me the best bang for my buck, calorically speaking, and I've found that you can still eat deliciously while accomplishing this goal. Healthy food can be really, really tasty, and when it is, you're happy eating it. For me, enjoying what I eat is key to getting me to eat it in the first place! Flavorful, healthful food that is prepared well, from whole and natural ingredients, does wonders for your soul, too. Plus, a resilient, tough spirit is mighty handy in world-class swimming.

Eating mindfully and with moderation is vitally important to a healthy lifestyle. I've come to know what my "fighting weight" is—that place where my physical makeup is ideal for competition. This is not my beach body or anything like that; it is my best bodily shape for performing at my highest level, and it comes from a combination of good eating, working out, and getting appropriate rest and recovery. Since I recognize that place so well, I know when I can handle an extra scoop of ice cream on my Halo Halo (page 212) or when to invite friends over to relax with a glass of wine and enjoy a hearty, cozy meal of Comfort Ragu (page 190). Or when I should stick to Thai-Style Butterfish en Papillote (page 157) and be extra diligent not to skip my Everyday Green Smoothie (page 194)! Giving yourself some grace to enjoy your favorite not-so-healthy treats every now and again is okay, provided it's all part of the larger balance. That said, it's all about making it count, so if you're going to indulge in pasta, for example, get the best-quality, most delicious pasta you can find!

Cook to Thrive is a collection of my personal recipes, from performance-rated dishes that I cooked when I was a competing Olympian to treasured family recipes for all occasions. This is how I regularly eat, so most of the dishes in these pages are healthy, but a few are less so (okay, and a handful really aren't healthy at all!). But I don't believe that there are "good" foods and "bad" foods, as long as it's all in moderation and balance. I've been lucky to have had lots of culinary influences in my life, first from my Filipino family, and then from growing up (and currently living) in San Francisco's Bay Area and attending college in Berkeley. The abundance of fresh, quality fruits and vegetables found year-round in Northern California is a daily inspiration that's reflected in the following pages. And the numerous countries I've traveled to during my swimming career have left an indelible mark on my palate and my trove of recipes—Spanish Tortilla (page 94) first tasted in Barcelona, Bircher Muesli (page 42) discovered in Australia, and Poisson Cru (page 160) enjoyed fresh from the sea in Polynesia, just to name a few. You'll find a touch of all these cuisines in this book.

HOW TO USE THIS BOOK

I'm a firm believer in starting the day with a good breakfast, too—whether in training mode or not. The first meal of the day is best if it's practical, so the recipes in the Breakfast chapter are healthy, tasty, quick, and easy, and most can be prepared ahead of time to "grab and go" in the morning.

The Salads & Soups and Vegetables chapters let fresh, seasonal produce really shine. Living in the Bay Area, I'm lucky to have top-notch fruits and vegetables available pretty much anywhere I go, and they inspire my cooking every day. No matter where you live, though, you'll be able to make these dishes because the ingredients can be found most anywhere. Seek out the freshest foods you can find, since they are the ones bursting with both flavor and nutrients. Charred Green Bean Salad (page 54), Smoky Gazpacho (page 70), Miso-Roasted Sweet Potatoes (page 84), Beets with Almonds and Orange-Scented Ricotta (page 66)—loading up on vegetable dishes is key to maximizing your nutrition intake, and the variety of spices, accompaniments, and preparations will ensure that you won't get bored with any of these recipes.

Since I need so many calories during training season, I've developed healthy Snacks & Bites to keep me from getting too hungry between meals. Avocado Cilantro Hummus (page 122) or a homemade spiced popcorn (page 134) always does the trick. I'm also a sports fan, and having Spinach Artichoke Dip (page 120) around at game time keeps me from overindulging.

My entrée chapters—Seafood and Meat & Poultry—primarily feature lean proteins, such as tilapia (page 152) and bison (page 169). But I also include a killer recipe for Pan-Seared Steak with Green Herb Sauce (page 164) and my mom's Chicken Adobo (page 178). Again, it's all about balance!

Finally, in Smoothies, Juices & Sweets, I share the drinks I reach for before, during, and after workouts, such as Performance Beet Juice (page 203), as well as an embellished version of a traditional Filipino cantaloupe juice (page 204) that also makes a fantastic summertime refreshment. Again, I've included some of Grandma's recipes here; her Filipino desserts are the ones I crave the most! For me, nothing satisfies that sweet craving like her Filipino Sticky Coconut Rice (page 209).

I'm fairly type A (that's a lie; I'm type A personified!), so I have found ways to organize my kitchen to maximize freshness and minimize waste. Throughout this book, you'll find practical information for freezing staples such as my Stir-Fry Sauce (page 88), selecting and preparing shellfish, and peeling a bunch of garlic without too much hassle. I've also given tips for selecting ripe fruits and vegetables, using a mortar and pestle (it's the best!), and dry-brining meats. And I've done my best to include ingredient substitutions, since I know that some of the Filipino items may be hard to find (though most Asian markets should have them).

Eating healthfully has played a significant role in my longevity as an athlete, and preparing food from scratch is a lifelong passion. I hope that you will find inspiration in these pages, and perhaps a new family favorite or two. Above all, my wish is to share the knowledge I've gained and the happiness I find in the kitchen. Food really is fuel—for all of us, whether we're athletes or not—but it can be life-giving in other ways when it's thoughtfully prepared and really, truly delicious!

HOW TO THRIVE FOR LIFE

So you're holding this fabulous cookbook full of nourishing recipes that will fill your week with delicious, vibrant meals. You're dedicated to eating better so you can feel great inside and out. Now you want to know how to stick with this lifestyle for the long run. Here's how.

1 ▪ **MAKE HEALTHY EATING A HABIT FOR LIFE.**

Experts say that it takes from a few weeks to a month to create a new habit. When you're starting out, force yourself to meal-plan and stick to a healthy diet. It'll be tough at first, but don't give up—this is about making a long-term change, and staying consistent and persistent at the start is key. Believe in the journey and the process. Once you've created this new habit, it will become second nature.

2 ▪ **FOCUS ON THE POSITIVES RATHER THAN THE NEGATIVES.**

Changing your diet for the better can be challenging, but it is much more enjoyable and achievable if you approach your goals with the right attitude. Instead of harping on about what you can't or shouldn't eat, think about getting all those good foods into your diet. Aim to eat as many nutrient-dense vegetables and fruits as possible, drink lots of water, and focus on healthy fats. This simple psychological shift makes a huge difference when aiming to eat better. It takes the focus away from depriving yourself of something and shifts it toward nourishing your body

3 ▪ **LISTEN TO YOUR BODY.**

Eat to feel good—inside and out. Pay attention to how you feel after a meal. Are you stuffed? Satisfied? Sluggish? Energized? Lethargic? I've always found that when I eat consciously, I gravitate toward the healthiest foods that sustain my active lifestyle.

4 ▪ **INDULGE FROM TIME TO TIME.**

One of the ways I sustain my healthy diet for life is by allowing myself occasional indulgences. Constant deprivation isn't sustainable or realistic—and let's face it, it's not very enjoyable!

When I do indulge, I make it count with foods that satisfy me in a wholly different way: rich Comfort Ragu (page 190) that I prepare for friends when I entertain, soulful Filipino dishes like Shrimp Fritters (page 148) and Sticky Coconut Rice (page 209) that remind me of my grandma, and Olive Fritte (page 121), which brings me back to my wedding day.

5 ▪ **MEAL-PLAN TO SET YOUR WEEK UP FOR SUCCESS.**

At the beginning of the week, spend twenty to thirty minutes planning the week's meals. Try to go to the grocery store once a week and no more. This will save you time and money while keeping you on the right track. Getting take-out is far less tempting when you have all the items for a healthy dinner waiting for you in the fridge. Nowadays there are also great apps for your phone that allow you to store recipes, meal-plan, and create grocery lists, making it even easier to stay on track.

6 ▪ A TIDY KITCHEN IS A HAPPY KITCHEN.

As I have mentioned, I'm kind of a type A personality. I love keeping my fridge, pantry, and kitchen organized and my cooking area clean as I prepare meals, and I encourage you to do the same. That little extra effort (see the tips on page 19) makes me feel calm and focused while I cook and plan meals. It takes the stress out of cooking, making it easy and even fun!

7 ▪ STAY HYDRATED.

We all know how important it is to stay hydrated. No matter how hydrated I am before I go to bed, I always seem to wake up parched. To get a jump on the day, I chug 20 ounces of water as soon as I wake up. From there on, I'll sip water throughout the day and easily consume the recommended amount. How much water should you drink? It can be anywhere between 60 and 100 ounces, depending on your weight, activity level, and the foods you ingest. Keep in mind that the foods you consume can aid hydration, but a rough goal to aim for is to drink half your weight in ounces. For instance, a 150-pound person should aim to drink 75 ounces of fluids. I often include frozen strawberries, frozen pineapple, fresh mint, fresh lemon verbena, or lemon slices in my water to add a hint of flavor.

8 ▪ BE PREPARED ON THE ROAD.

I have always believed in keeping an "emergency pack" of healthy snacks with me at all times. This is especially important when I travel. Disrupted sleep schedules and stress from traveling increase your cortisol levels, which ultimately affect your appetite. Rather than being at the mercy of whatever is available, I always have a zip-top bag with nuts, dried fruit, herbal tea bags, and dark chocolate with me. This combination always satisfies my cravings and allows me to stay on track.

9 ▪ THINK OF YOUR GREEN SMOOTHIE AS A DAILY VITAMIN.

The easiest way to incorporate nutrient-dense foods into your diet is with smoothies. A daily green smoothie (see page 194) helps me consume a large amount of raw, leafy greens in an easy, portable way. I love a big salad, but sometimes I just don't have the time to sit down to eat one. With a smoothie, I have no excuses.

10 ▪ PACK IN THE PROTEIN.

Protein is essential to a healthy diet, and consuming your daily requirement of protein throughout the day not only helps stave off hunger but also has been shown to be the most efficient way to support muscle growth, maintenance, and repair. Instead of having a huge helping of protein at dinner or lunch, aim to have a bit of protein with all your meals, including snacks. Take some time to educate yourself on the sources of protein: protein doesn't just mean meat. There is protein in yogurt, nuts, eggs, dark leafy greens, legumes, and more.

BACK TO BASICS

PANTRY AND FRIDGE ESSENTIALS

Keeping a well-stocked fridge, freezer, and pantry is key to making cooking healthy foods at home easy and approachable any day of the week.

1 ▪ CLEAR OUT AND CLEAN YOUR FRIDGE BEFORE HEADING TO THE GROCERY STORE.

A clean, organized fridge allows you to quickly find what you need while sparking creativity for your week's meals. Use up items that are approaching their expiration date and discard or compost the items that are no longer edible. Leftover proteins and grains can be added to tomorrow's lunch salad. Utilize those bits and ends in a stir-fry (see page 86) or frittata (see pages 28 and 30). Cleaning out your fridge will also force you to take inventory of what you have on hand so that you don't end up buying duplicates, which often leads to waste.

2 ▪ YOUR FREEZER IS YOUR FRIEND.

Take time to organize, label, and date the items in your freezer. Take inventory at least once a month and use up anything that is coming close to its expiration (I usually use the rough guidelines from the FDA: stocks for 3 to 6 months, meats for up to 1 year, and prepared leftovers for 3 months). When defrosting items, the gentlest way is to simply place them in the fridge and let them slowly defrost overnight. This does the least amount of damage to the cell structure of the food and doesn't negatively affect its texture. The next best way to defrost an item is with a cold-water bath: fill a large bowl with cold water and place the frozen item (sealed in a zip-top bag with the air pressed out) in the water; change the water frequently until the item is defrosted.

3 ▪ COOK PANTRY ITEMS IN BULK ON WEEKENDS.

Spend a bit of time on the weekend to cook up a large pot of whole grains, oatmeal, and/or dried beans for the week. These nutrient-dense items can take some time to cook, but it's mostly hands-off. Beans and grains add substance and can turn a simple salad into a filling meal.

4 ▪ KEEP YOUR SPICE CABINET ORGANIZED.

Invest in small glass jars for spices and keep them organized. Once you begin to accumulate various spices they can get lost in the cabinet if they aren't properly organized. Spend ten minutes arranging your spices in alphabetical order so you can quickly find the one you want. I like to buy the spices that come in small cardboard boxes and decant them into my jars. This way, I'm not buying too much, which ensures that my spices are always fresh.

Once your fridge is clear and your pantry is organized, here's how you stock them:

Pantry

QUALITY OLIVE OIL   When you are finishing a dish or making salad dressing or an herb oil, the difference in flavor between a great olive oil and a cheap one is remarkable. There are plenty of affordable, quality options out there. You don't need to break the bank.

HIGH-HEAT NEUTRAL OILS   Oils that have a high smoking point are perfect for methods such as stir-frying. My favorite is grapeseed due to its clean flavor, but canola, avocado, sunflower, and other vegetable oils are fine substitutes.

SOY SAUCE   I prefer high-quality, gluten-free tamari because it is free of unnecessary additives. It adds a wonderful salty punch of umami to almost any dish that needs a bit of salt.

FINISHING SALT   My personal favorite for finishing is Maldon sea salt. A quality flaky sea salt like Maldon makes all the difference when finishing your salads, veggies, meats, and more. The pop of salt and texture is simply divine.

WHOLE PEPPERCORNS   Tellicherry peppercorns are my favorite type of black pepper to freshly grind. They are more fragrant than regular black peppercorns and add a more nuanced pepper flavor.

Fridge and Freezer

EGGS   I started keeping chickens almost a decade ago because I understood that eggs are a great source of affordable quality protein. I wholeheartedly agree that almost every dish—whether for breakfast, lunch, or dinner—is better with an egg on top. The unctuous richness of a runny egg yolk is a sauce that cannot be beat.

FRESH HERBS   Fresh herbs add a ton of flavor to a variety of dishes without adding unnecessary calories. Store sprigs of delicate fresh herbs such as cilantro or basil as you would a bouquet of fresh flowers: snip off the bottoms, quickly wash and dry the herbs, and then store them in a small jar with a bit of water at the bottom. I store basil in the window at room temperature, but cilantro often prefers the fridge. You can also loosely wrap a plastic bag around the top of the jar to keep in the humidity, but the herbs will keep without it. This process may take a bit of time, but purchasing fresh herbs can be quite costly, and this ensures that they'll last if you aren't planning on using the whole bunch right away, so you'll get the most out of them.

FRESH CHILE PEPPERS   I absolutely love heat in my food. Whether I'm making a spicy pesto or a fresh salsa, a little bit of chile goes a long way. Store fresh chiles in a sealed zip-top bag in the crisper drawer of the fridge; they should last for two to three weeks. Wash the chiles right before you plan on cooking them.

HOMEMADE CHICKEN STOCK   Whether you're making a soup, risotto, or simple pan sauce, having flavorful chicken stock in the freezer is a lifesaver. I like to freeze chicken stock in ice cube trays and then transfer them to a plastic freezer bag; I also freeze quart-size amounts directly in freezer bags. Having a supply of premeasured stock in the freezer saves time when you're preparing a last-minute meal.

NUTS   I always buy nuts in bulk and store them in the freezer. Many nuts are quite expensive, and you don't want to find that they have gone rancid in your kitchen cabinet. Freeze them in glass jars or plastic freezer bags to keep them fresh for as long as possible.

CASTELVETRANO OLIVES   Whether I'm simply craving a salty snack or need a punch of flavor for a variety of dishes, these are my favorite olives to have on hand. Not only are they packed with rich, nuanced flavor, but, like all olives, they are also full of omega-3 fatty acids.

STRAINED YOGURT   I love snacking on strained yogurt, especially Icelandic yogurt. Icelandic yogurt is made in the same way as Greek yogurt, but it is often strained a bit longer, resulting in even thicker yogurt with a higher protein content. It's very low in sugar but satisfyingly rich.

BASIC TOOLS AND EQUIPMENT

Most of my recipes don't require much equipment. Here's a list of my "must-have" kitchen tools, along with some equipment that I love to have on hand but that isn't 100 percent essential.

Must-Haves

THREE KNIVES: CHEF'S, SERRATED, AND PARING Having a sharp chef's knife that feels good in your hand can make so much difference in preparation time! Invest in a great knife and take good care of it. There's no need to have an entire butcher block of knives. A paring knife for small tasks, a serrated knife for cutting bread, and an all-purpose chef's knife are all you need.

CUTTING BOARDS I like to keep three cutting boards on hand: one as the main cutting board, one for non-savory items, and one for raw meats and fish. The main cutting board is your workhorse for all your vegetable prep and more. Use it often and take great care of it. If it's wood, make sure to oil it often with food-grade oil, such as mineral oil. The non-savory board is for sweeter items such as fruit or bread, or anything else that you may not want affected by lingering garlic or onion flavor. The raw meat cutting board (I prefer a plastic board for this) is only for preparing raw poultry, meat, or fish. Once you have cooked that meat, poultry, or fish, sanitize this board immediately to avoid spreading any harmful bacteria throughout your kitchen. To sanitize, I immediately put my plastic board in the dishwasher after using. For a wooden cutting board (or another board

that can't handle the dishwasher) spread 3% hydrogen peroxide over the board with a clean sponge or paper towel. Allow the hydrogen peroxide to sit for a few minutes, then rinse with water and dry.

A STACK OF DISH TOWELS Keeping your prep station clean makes cooking much more enjoyable. When you're preparing a meal, have a clean, damp dish towel nearby to wipe off your cutting board or chef's knife—it makes preparing recipes so much easier. While you're at it, clean as you go. It saves you a lot of time, to say nothing of fatigue, when you don't have a daunting stack of dirty dishes waiting for you in the kitchen at the end of a meal.

LARGE STOCKPOT If you plan on making homemade stock (see page 68), doubling or tripling the recipe uses the same amount of effort—all you need is a stockpot that's large enough to accommodate all the ingredients. Aim to buy at least a 12-quart stockpot.

DUTCH OVEN You can certainly use your stockpot to cook stews and soups, but it can be a bit larger than necessary. If you have the funds and the room for another pot, I would get a 6- to 8-quart pot, ideally an enameled cast-iron Dutch oven.

CAST-IRON PAN If you take proper care of a cast-iron pan, it will last you a lifetime. I have collected several antique cast-iron pans over the years and stripped and reseasoned them (see opposite). Now they're my go-to nonstick pans without the worry of the harmful chemicals found in Teflon or similar nonstick coatings. Plus, I don't have to worry about scratching them while cooking. Cast iron is nearly indestructible.

HIGH-POWERED BLENDER When it comes to making a green smoothie, nothing beats a Vitamix. This powerful blender completely liquefies the fibrous stems of kale and other dark leafy greens and transforms them into an easily digestible smoothie. While a Vitamix or comparable blender can be very expensive, refurbished models are available and are a great option. Standard blenders can work in a pinch, but they won't completely break down fibrous vegetables like kale.

DIGITAL INSTANT-READ THERMOMETER Instead of trying to guess whether your chicken, fish, or steak is done, invest $10 in an instant-read thermometer so you can easily achieve that perfect medium-rare.

FREEZER TAPE AND PERMANENT MARKER Rather than play the "Is it safe to eat?" guessing game with foods, simply label and date items as they go into your fridge or freezer.

COMMERCIAL-GRADE HALF-SHEET PANS Do yourself a favor and purchase heavy-duty commercial half-sheet pans. I made the mistake of buying cheap ones when I first started cooking, and I

HOW TO RESEASON A CAST-IRON PAN

If your pan has lost its coating, reseasoning a cast-iron pan takes a bit of time and effort, but you will be rewarded in the end. The most foolproof method I've found for reseasoning pans is from blogger Sheryl Canter. First, open the windows and turn on the kitchen fan because there will likely be a lot of smoke. Put your cast-iron pan in the oven and turn the oven to self-cleaning mode.

After the self-cleaning cycle has finished (2 to 3 hours) and the cast-iron pan has cooled, wash the pan with dish soap and water. Towel-dry the pan and then place it in a 200°F oven for 15 minutes to dry fully. The self-cleaning cycle has stripped away the pan's coating, so it is crucial to get this pan bone-dry before it starts rusting.

Take a tablespoon or two of flaxseed oil and rub it all over the warm dried pan. Then, using an old dish towel or a paper towel, rub off all the oil. Since cast-iron pans are porous, you won't actually rub off *all* the oil—some will have soaked in—but this is a very important step that ensures you'll be left with a rock-hard, slick surface, rather than a sticky coating.

Once you have rubbed off all the excess oil, place the pan in the oven and set it to 500°F or as high as it will go. Once the oven reaches that temperature, set the timer for 1 hour.

After that 1 hour, turn the oven off but do not open the oven. Leave the pan to cool in the oven for at least 2 hours. Repeat the oiling, heating, and cooling process several times until the pan develops a smooth sheen.

regretted it because they bent and warped after just a little use. Sheet pans are one of those kitchen items that I use beyond their intended design. Of course you can use them for roasting, such as in Yogurt-Roasted Carrots (page 101) or Sheet Pan Tilapia (page 152), but you can also use them as a work surface when seasoning a lot of items at once, as a tray to carry your *mise en place* to your outdoor grill, or as a place to rest cooked meats.

OVEN-SAFE WIRE RACK   Cooking foods on a wire rack set over a sheet pan allows more air circulation than a sheet pan without a rack. I use wire racks to wick away all the excess oil when I'm frying Grandma's Lumpia (page 128), to season my strip steak for Pan-Seared Steak with Green Herb Sauce (page 164), and to season the chicken for my Roasted Chicken Legs with Kabocha Squash (page 184). They take little storage room (just store them nested within your sheet pans).

Nice-to-Haves

MORTAR AND PESTLE   It can seem silly to use a mortar and pestle when a food processor is available, but I assure you that there is a huge difference in texture (and even taste) in the final product. While a food processor chops food into tiny pieces, a mortar and pestle pounds the food and extracts all the essential oils, resulting in creamier pestos and sauces. If you're using a mortar and pestle to grind spices or nuts, the results have more textural variety, which is more interesting to the palate.

DIGITAL SCALE   A digital scale doesn't cost much and it makes measuring a cinch when you can zero out the scale with the push of a button, allowing for the weight of your container. Many ingredients, dry ingredients especially, are more accurately measured by weight than by volume.

VACUUM SEALER   Prevent ice crystals from forming on your frozen food by using a vacuum sealer. If something is on sale at the butcher shop but I'm not ready to cook it, I'll seal it airtight with a vacuum sealer and keep it in the freezer until I'm ready to enjoy it. It saves me money and lets me avoid wasting food.

RECIPE CHEAT SHEET

A quick reference for when you're looking for
a recipe to satisfy just the right situation.

PRE-WORKOUT

To feel energized before
your workout

Breakfast Fried Rice, page 32
Steel-Cut Oatmeal with Seasonal
Compotes, page 36

Bircher Muesli, page 42
Peanut Butter Energy Bites, page 137
Strawberry Oat Smoothie, page 201
Performance Beet Juice, page 203

POST-WORKOUT

To feel replenished
after your workout

Cherry-Almond Recovery
Smoothie, page 197

Water
Watermelon Slushie, page 198
Lentil Caprese, page 61

ON-THE-GO

To grab and go when
you're on the run

Hummus-Avocado Collard
Green Wraps, page 102
Everyday Green Smoothie, page 194
Cherry-Almond Recovery
Smoothie, page 197

Mango Coconut Smoothie, page 202
Strawberry Oat Smoothie, page 201
Peanut Butter Energy Bites, page 137

PARTY SNACKS

Better-for-you bites for snacking
with friends and family

Mango Guacamole, page 124
Avocado Cilantro Hummus, page 122
Roasted Piquillo Pepper and
Garlic Hummus, page 125

Spinach Artichoke Dip, page 120
Spicy "Cheesy" Popcorn, page 134

IN RECORD TIME

For when you want to make
dinner but have no time

Lazy Ramen, page 78
Thai-Style Butterfish en Papillote, page 157
Spicy Coconut Mussels, page 140

Longanisa Steamer Clams, page 144
Pan-Seared Steak with Green
Herb Sauce, page 164
Sheet Pan Tilapia
with Cherry Salsa, page 152

MAKE AHEAD

Dishes that can be prepared
or cooked ahead of time

Shredded Brussels Sprouts and Kale Salad
with Pomegranate and Cranberries, page 63
Bison Shepherd's Pie, page 169
Chicken Adobo, page 178
Slow Cooker Coq au Vin, page 182

Comfort Ragu, page 190
Filipino Ham Hock Soup, page 76
Restorative Garlic Soup, page 74
Lazy Ramen, page 78

NOURISH AND INDULGE

For when you want a touch
of decadence, whether
savory or sweet

Grandma's Lumpia, page 128
Olive Fritte, page 121
Shrimp Fritters, page 148
Comfort Ragu, page 190

Pork Schnitzel with Red Cabbage
Apple Slaw, page 171
Filipino Sticky Coconut Rice, page 209
Halo Halo, page 212
Dessert Lumpia, page 214

BREAKFAST

ASPARAGUS AND SWEET ONION FRITTATA

■ SERVES 4 TO 6 Since I started raising chickens, I have made frittatas at least once a week. If you have some eggs on hand and want to clear out your fridge, make a frittata! The basic technique is simple: prepare vegetables and fillings, spread them evenly in a skillet, top with well-beaten eggs, and finish cooking in the oven. This recipe is for an asparagus version, but there are endless possibilities—broccoli and sharp cheddar (see page 30); tomato, corn, and basil; roasted bell pepper and feta; even leftover spaghetti makes a wonderful frittata. They are delicious warm, at room temperature, or cold. Serve a frittata with a green salad, and you have an easy-to-prepare light dinner.

1 pound asparagus, trimmed

2 tablespoons extra-virgin olive oil

Kosher salt and freshly ground black pepper

10 large eggs

1 (5.2-ounce) package Garlic & Herb Boursin cheese

1 tablespoon unsalted butter

1 large sweet onion, such as Vidalia, thinly sliced (about 2½ cups)

1. Preheat the oven to 425°F.

2. Place the asparagus on a rimmed baking sheet and drizzle with 1 tablespoon of the olive oil. Season with a hefty pinch each of salt and pepper. Roast until the spears are cooked through but still have some bite, about 10 minutes (if the spears are quite fat, you may need to cook them longer). Remove from the oven and let cool slightly. Coarsely chop the asparagus into bite-size pieces.

3. Reduce the oven temperature to 300°F.

4. In a large bowl, whisk together the eggs, 3 tablespoons of the Boursin cheese, ½ teaspoon salt, and ½ teaspoon pepper (the Boursin will be pretty chunky; don't worry about whisking it smooth).

5. Heat a large cast-iron or other ovenproof skillet over medium heat. Add the butter and remaining 1 tablespoon olive oil to the pan. When the foaming subsides, add the onion. Cook, stirring occasionally, until the onion is translucent and soft, about 5 minutes. Add the asparagus and the egg mixture to the skillet and cook, undisturbed, for 1 minute.

6. Transfer the skillet to the oven and bake until the eggs are just barely set and jiggle slightly when you shake the pan, 20 to 25 minutes. Remove the pan from the oven and use an offset spatula or a knife to release the frittata from the sides of the pan.

7. Let the frittata cool for 5 minutes before transferring it to a large platter. Slice it into wedges and slather a tablespoon of the Boursin on each slice before serving.

ROASTED BROCCOLI AND CHEDDAR FRITTATA

■ SERVES 4 TO 6   Here is another one of my favorite ways to make a
frittata. While most people discard their broccoli stems, I peel and roast
them to include right alongside the florets. They add more broccoli flavor,
not to mention an extra dose of healthy vitamins and minerals. I like
to include a touch of red pepper flakes for some spice. Be sure to use a
high-quality sharp cheddar cheese—the gooey topping will be all the more
delicious for it.

1½ pounds broccoli

3 tablespoons olive oil

Kosher salt and freshly
ground black pepper

10 large eggs

1 large onion, thinly
sliced (about 2 cups)

¼ teaspoon crushed red
pepper flakes (optional)

⅔ cup shredded sharp
cheddar cheese

1. Preheat the oven to 450°F.

2. Cut the thick stems off the broccoli heads and set them
   aside. Divide the broccoli heads into small florets. Using a
   vegetable peeler, peel and discard the tough outer layer
   from the broccoli stems, then slice the stems into very
   thin coins.

3. On a rimmed baking sheet, toss the sliced broccoli stems
   with 1 tablespoon of the olive oil, season with salt and
   black pepper, and spread out into an even layer. On a
   separate rimmed baking sheet, toss the broccoli florets
   with 1 tablespoon of the olive oil, season with salt and
   black pepper, and spread out into an even layer. Place
   both baking sheets in the oven and roast, stirring halfway
   through, until the broccoli is tender and browned in
   parts, about 15 minutes. Remove from the oven and let
   cool slightly.

4. Reduce the oven temperature to 300°F.

5. In a large bowl, whisk together the eggs, 1 teaspoon salt,
   and ½ teaspoon black pepper until smooth.

6. Heat a large cast-iron or other ovenproof skillet over medium heat. Add the remaining 1 tablespoon olive oil and the onion. Cook, stirring occasionally, until the onion is very soft and slightly caramelized, about 15 minutes. Add the red pepper flakes, if using, and cook for 1 more minute. Add the roasted broccoli stems and florets, stir well, and spread the vegetables evenly in the skillet. Pour the egg mixture over the vegetables and use a spatula to spread it out evenly. Sprinkle the cheddar on top and cook, undisturbed, for 1 minute.

7. Transfer the skillet to the oven. Bake until the eggs are just barely set and jiggle slightly when you shake the pan, 20 to 25 minutes. Remove the pan from the oven and use an offset spatula or a knife to release the frittata from the sides of the pan.

8. Let the frittata cool for 5 minutes before transferring it to a large platter. Slice it into wedges and serve.

BREAKFAST FRIED RICE

■ SERVES 2 OR 3   Eating meals during athletic competition, especially when traveling, can be a challenge. Often you're faced with unfamiliar food when you need something reliable to fuel your body for the day. Fortunately, my breakfast of choice was almost always available. Whether I was at the Olympics, World Championships, or Pan American Games, I could reliably find rice, eggs, and soy sauce.

Leftover rice mixed with lots of garlic, veggies, and eggs is actually a common Filipino breakfast called *sinangag*. Rather than fry the eggs in a separate pan, I like to cook them directly in little craters that I make in the rice mixture. My version uses collard greens, which I love because they become silky during cooking while providing you with all sorts of nutrients and minerals. But feel free to substitute other vegetables that strike your fancy.

1 bunch collard greens

1 tablespoon plus 1½ teaspoons grapeseed oil or other high-heat neutral oil (see page 20)

8 garlic cloves, minced

2 tablespoons soy sauce or tamari, plus more for serving

3 cups leftover cooked rice (brown, white, or a combination; see Note)

6 large eggs

3 scallions, green parts only, thinly sliced

1. Set an oven rack 6 to 8 inches from the heating element and preheat the broiler.

2. Cut out and discard the ribs of the collard greens. Stack the collard leaves on top of one another and, starting on a long side, roll them up into a burrito-like shape. Thinly slice the rolled greens crosswise into ribbons, then coarsely chop the ribbons so that they are not too long.

3. Heat a large oven-safe skillet, such as cast iron, over medium-high heat. When the skillet is hot, add 1 tablespoon of the grapeseed oil and the garlic. Cook, stirring constantly, until the garlic is a light golden color and very fragrant, about 1 minute. Do not let it burn. Add the collard greens, 1 tablespoon of the soy sauce, and ¼ cup water. Cook, stirring, until the collard greens are wilted and all the liquid has evaporated, about 8 minutes.

4. Add the rice and the remaining 1 tablespoon soy sauce to the collard greens. Cook, stirring, until the rice has warmed, 2 minutes. Spread the mixture out evenly in the skillet and make six wells with a spoon. Pour ¼ teaspoon of the remaining grapeseed oil into each well and then carefully crack an egg into each well. Cook, undisturbed, until the egg whites are beginning to set, about 1 minute. Transfer the skillet to the oven and broil until the eggs are cooked to your desired doneness. (I prefer just-set whites and runny yolks, which takes about 1 minute.)

5. Remove the skillet from the oven and sprinkle the scallions over the rice and eggs. Serve immediately, with soy sauce on the side.

LEFTOVER RICE   Fried rice is meant to be a convenience food that utilizes and gives new life to leftovers. Leftover rice is actually preferred when making fried rice because it is slightly dried out and holds up to frying better. If you want to make this dish using freshly cooked rice, simply spread the rice out on a baking sheet and place it in the fridge, uncovered, for 30 minutes to dry out.

Breakfast Fried Rice

STEEL-CUT OATMEAL

WITH SEASONAL COMPOTES

■ SERVES 4 During training seasons, very early mornings were always a part of my routine. I often hit the water at 6 a.m., which means I got to the pool at 5:15 a.m. or so to begin my preparation work, and that means my wake-up call was somewhere around 4:30 a.m. Skipping breakfast was never an option. When you're working out for hours on end, you need to eat something nutritious first thing in order to keep your energy levels stable. And making breakfast that early in the morning had to be easy. But just because it was easy didn't mean it wasn't delicious!

On Sundays, I would make a big pot of steel-cut oats, transfer the cooked oatmeal to a glass container, and keep it in the fridge for a week's worth of breakfasts. Regular steel-cut oats (not the quick-cook variety) are filled with fiber, protein, and whole grains—and they're easy to digest, too, which is especially important before a two-hour swim session. But as nutritious as they are, they can be a bit boring on their own, so I came up with some flavorful toppings. I also add ground flaxseed (for fiber and omega-3 fatty acids) and coconut oil (for medium-chain triglycerides) to boost the overall nutrition of my oatmeal.

I've also included recipes for three of my favorite compotes to eat with oatmeal. They can be made ahead, too: Once you've made the toppings, refrigerate them until cool. Then transfer them to an ice cube tray and freeze until solid. Pop the compote blocks into a plastic zip-top bag, label and date it, and store it in the freezer for up to 6 months. When you're ready to eat your breakfast, scoop some oatmeal into a microwavable bowl and add a cube or two of compote. Microwave until warm, and enjoy! We all need things that make us happy in the morning, even at 5 a.m. This is one of them.

---

1 cup steel-cut oats

Kosher salt

1 to 2 tablespoons extra-virgin coconut oil, to taste

¼ cup ground flaxseed

Compote (page 37, 38, or 40), for serving

1. Bring 4 cups water to a boil in a medium saucepan. When the water is boiling, whisk in the steel-cut oats and reduce the heat to medium-low. Add a heavy pinch of salt and cook, stirring occasionally, until the oats are cooked through and have absorbed all the water, 20 to 25 minutes. Add the coconut oil and ground flaxseed and cook for 1 minute more, stirring to incorporate them into the mixture.

2. Serve immediately with your choice of compote on top, or let the oatmeal cool and then transfer it to a resealable container. The cooled oatmeal will keep in the fridge for up to 1 week.

BANANA BROWN BUTTER

■ MAKES ABOUT 2 CUPS My mom made something very similar to this when I was a kid. She would cook extra-ripe bananas with a little sugar and cinnamon until they had a jammy consistency, and I loved to eat it on top of French toast. In my version, I first brown the butter to give it a rich, nutty flavor that tastes almost decadent with the sweet bananas. I'll often throw some walnuts or pecans into my oatmeal bowl, too, for more nut flavor and some crunch (not to mention the extra fiber and omega-3s!).

2 tablespoons unsalted butter

5 very ripe bananas, mashed

¼ teaspoon ground cinnamon, or more to taste

Kosher salt

In a small saucepan (a light-colored pan is best so that you can see the butter change color as it cooks), melt the butter over medium heat. Swirl the butter around in the pan as it bubbles up, using a spoon to skim off and discard any white foam that collects on the top. Continue to cook the butter, swirling the pan occasionally. Keep a close eye on it because the browning process happens quickly. After about 5 minutes, the butter will turn a golden brown color and smell nutty. Quickly add the bananas, cinnamon, and ¼ teaspoon salt. Cook, stirring occasionally, until the bananas melt into the butter, about 5 minutes. At this point, you can leave the banana butter as is or pulse it in a small food processor for a smoother consistency. Taste and add more cinnamon if you like.

PEACHES AND CREAM

■ MAKES ABOUT 2 CUPS My grandparents have two mature peach trees that produce a bumper crop every summer. It's impossible to keep up with the supply. I'll freeze some for smoothies, grill some more for a salad (see page 52), and make this peach compote. If you don't have a supply of fresh peaches or simply do not want to bother peeling them, feel free to substitute peeled frozen peaches (about 3 cups) and add about 5 minutes to the overall cooking time.

5 ripe peaches

1½ teaspoons light brown sugar, or more to taste

Kosher salt

1 tablespoon vanilla paste or extract (see Note)

1 tablespoon heavy cream

1. To peel the peaches, bring a large pot of water to a boil over high heat. Prepare a large bowl of ice water and place it nearby. Using a small knife, score the skin of each peach by cutting an X in the bottom (the size of the X doesn't really matter). When the water is at a rolling boil, add the peaches. Boil for 60 seconds, then immediately transfer them to the ice water to cool.

2. When the peaches are cool enough to handle, use your fingers to pull the skins off; they should slide off easily. Cut the peeled peaches in half. Remove and discard the

Roasted Strawberry-Rhubarb Compote

Banana Brown Butter

Peaches and Cream

pits. Coarsely chop the peaches into chunks (you should have about 3 cups) and put them in a small saucepan. Add 2 tablespoons water and set the pan over medium-low heat. Cook, stirring occasionally, until the peaches start releasing their liquid, about 2 minutes, then stir in the brown sugar and a generous pinch of salt. Cook, stirring occasionally, until the peaches are very soft, 10 to 15 minutes.

3. Using a potato masher or a fork, mash the peaches in the saucepan until they are mostly broken up. Cook, stirring occasionally, until the compote has reduced to about 2 cups, 5 to 10 minutes.

4. Remove the pan from the heat. Stir in the vanilla and taste for seasoning. Depending on the ripeness of the peaches, you may want to add another 1½ teaspoons brown sugar. Stir in the heavy cream.

VANILLA PASTE   Ever since I discovered vanilla paste and tasted its superior flavor, I rarely use vanilla extract. You can find the paste in quality grocery stores, but if you can't find it, substitute vanilla extract.

ROASTED STRAWBERRY-RHUBARB COMPOTE

■ MAKES ABOUT 2 CUPS   Few things scream "spring" more than the combination of strawberries and rhubarb. Unlike many compote recipes that are overwhelmingly sweet, this one has only a touch of sweetness so the tart rhubarb still shines. When strawberries are at their peak, make a big batch of this compote to freeze (see page 36) for future use.

2 cups strawberries, hulled and sliced ¼-inch thick

1 large stalk rhubarb, cut into ½-inch cubes (2 cups)

2 tablespoons sugar

Kosher salt

½ teaspoon grated lemon zest (from ¼ lemon)

1. Preheat the oven to 375°F.

2. In a 9 x 13-inch baking dish, toss together the strawberries, rhubarb, and sugar. Roast, stirring once or twice, until the strawberries and rhubarb are thoroughly softened, 20 minutes.

3. Transfer the mixture to a small food processor, add ⅛ teaspoon salt and the lemon zest, and pulse a few times, until there are still some chunks remaining, or to your preferred consistency.

BIRCHER MUESLI

■ **SERVES 6 TO 8**   Bircher muesli, also known as "overnight oats," is the perfect breakfast for anyone wanting a healthy start to their day without much effort. I like to use a combination of rolled oats and steel-cut oats to create varying textures, but feel free to use just rolled oats if you prefer.

This breakfast will forever remind me of my first National Team trip to the Pan Pacific Swimming Championships in Sydney, Australia, when I was sixteen years old. I had never heard of bircher muesli before, but our hotel's breakfast buffet had a big bowl of it, and I thought it tasted like cookie dough. What a nice surprise to find out that it's actually quite healthful!

2 cups thick-cut old-fashioned rolled oats (I like Bob's Red Mill) or regular old-fashioned rolled oats

½ cup steel-cut oats

2 tablespoons chia seeds (see Note)

½ cup raisins

3 tablespoons unsweetened coconut flakes (optional)

3 cups almond milk

¼ cup maple syrup

1 teaspoon vanilla paste or extract (see Note, page 39)

1 teaspoon ground cinnamon

¼ teaspoon freshly grated nutmeg

Kosher salt

1 cup walnuts, toasted (see Note) and coarsely chopped

Sliced banana, for serving (optional)

Fresh blueberries, for serving (optional)

1. In a large bowl, combine the rolled oats, steel-cut oats, chia seeds, raisins, and coconut flakes, if using.

2. In a medium bowl, whisk together the almond milk, maple syrup, vanilla, cinnamon, nutmeg, and ½ teaspoon salt. Pour the almond milk mixture over the oat mixture and stir well. Let it sit for 10 minutes, then stir again to ensure the chia seeds don't clump together. Cover and let soak in the refrigerator overnight.

3. The next day, give the muesli a good stir, then scoop it into serving bowls. Top with the walnuts and add banana slices and/or blueberries, if you like. The muesli will keep in an airtight container in the refrigerator for up to 1 week.

CHIA SEEDS Chia seeds are packed with fiber and omega-3 fatty acids. They plump up quite a bit when added to liquid so they aid in hydration while keeping you satiated. After purchasing, keep chia seeds in the fridge.

TOASTED NUTS AND SEEDS Toasting seeds and nuts is fast and simple: Heat the seeds or nuts in a dry skillet over medium-low heat, stirring occasionally (and flipping if the nuts are large) and watching closely. They're ready when they become fragrant and are lightly browned, 3 to 5 minutes for seeds and 5 to 7 minutes for nuts. Immediately pour the nuts or seeds onto a plate to cool.

SALADS & SOUPS

BALSAMIC VINAIGRETTE

■ MAKES ABOUT 1¼ CUPS If there is one thing that I refuse to buy at the grocery store, it's prepared salad dressing. It may be considered a convenience item, but the fact is, dressing couldn't be simpler to make yourself—and it tastes way better and is free of unnecessary preservatives and fillers. The traditional way to make salad dressing is by slowly whisking olive oil into an acid base (vinegar or lemon juice, for example) to ensure a beautiful emulsion. But I like to dump everything into a jar and shake it vigorously—not quite as romantic as the traditional method, but it works just as well and eliminates an extra dirty dish to wash. Win-win, in my opinion!

I make this basic balsamic vinaigrette on a weekly basis. It's really a suggested ratio rather than a recipe, as vinaigrettes are generally 3 parts olive oil to 1 part vinegar (if you like your vinaigrette more acidic, feel free to adjust). Depending on my mood, I either use shallots or garlic—the shallots are a little less pungent than the garlic—so feel free to substitute one for the other. And you can also add an array of herbs and spices or swap in different vinegars to make any number of flavor variations. Two of my favorites are white wine vinegar with fresh chervil and red wine vinegar with pureed roasted tomatoes. This is the time to use that high-quality extra-virgin olive oil so its superior flavor can shine.

My favorite salad to use this dressing with is a spring lettuce mix with toasted walnuts, sliced fresh strawberries, and Fromager d'Affinois blue cheese.

¾ cup extra-virgin olive oil

⅓ cup balsamic vinegar

1 tablespoon Dijon mustard

1 teaspoon honey

1½ tablespoons minced shallot, or 1½ teaspoons minced garlic

⅛ teaspoon crushed red pepper flakes, plus more as needed

Kosher salt and freshly ground black pepper

In a 16-ounce mason jar or similar lidded glass jar, combine the olive oil, vinegar, mustard, honey, shallot, red pepper flakes, ⅛ teaspoon salt, and ¼ teaspoon black pepper. Shake vigorously until well combined. Taste and season with more red pepper flakes, salt, and/or black pepper as desired. Keep in mind that salad greens have a lot of water in them, which will mellow out the vinaigrette's flavor. The vinaigrette will keep in an airtight container in the refrigerator for up to 1 week.

FIG WINE DRESSING

■ MAKES ABOUT ½ CUP Figs have long been one of my favorite fruits. When I was young, I lived near a state park where my sister and I would ride our bikes while our dad ran alongside us. In the late summer and early fall, our treat at the end of the bike ride was picking fruit from the giant fig tree rooted at the end of the trail. I've been hooked ever since. A Black Mission fig tree was one of the first trees that I planted in my backyard, followed by two more varieties: Panache and Violette de Bordeaux.

This recipe draws out the savory side of figs. The juicy fruit is cooked down to a jam with red wine and fresh thyme, and then blended with piquant balsamic vinegar and aromatic shallots. Beautiful in a salad, it's also wonderful as a sauce for grilled meats or an accompaniment for a cheese plate. My salad of choice: sliced fresh figs, caramelized onions, and Gorgonzola cheese over mixed chicory greens.

½ cup chopped fresh Black Mission figs (about 5 figs)

¼ cup dry red wine

1 teaspoon minced fresh thyme

Freshly ground black pepper

2 tablespoons balsamic vinegar

1 tablespoon minced shallot

⅓ cup extra-virgin olive oil

Kosher salt

1. In a small saucepan set over medium heat, combine the figs, wine, thyme, and ½ teaspoon pepper. Bring the mixture to a boil and reduce the heat to maintain a simmer. Cook until there is little liquid left, the figs have broken down, and the mixture is jammy, 8 to 10 minutes.

2. Transfer the mixture to a small food processor or blender and add the vinegar and shallot. Process until smooth. With the motor running, drizzle in the olive oil and process until it is fully incorporated. Taste and season with salt and more pepper as desired.

LEMON YOGURT DRESSING

■ MAKES 1¾ CUPS   Here's another super-simple salad dressing that I make all the time. It's very creamy thanks to the yogurt, and the lemon and chives are bright and refreshing. My favorite salad for this dressing is mixed greens with shaved fennel, orange suprêmes, and chopped Castelvetrano olives. The buttery green olives and sweet orange sections contrast perfectly with the tangy dressing. You'll find this dressing is really versatile, though, and even makes a great dip for crudités.

1 cup full-fat yogurt (not Greek)

1 tablespoon finely grated lemon zest (from about 1 lemon)

1½ tablespoons fresh lemon juice (from about ½ lemon)

½ cup extra-virgin olive oil

1 tablespoon honey

1 tablespoon finely chopped fresh chives

Kosher salt and freshly ground black pepper

In a medium bowl, whisk together the yogurt, lemon zest, and lemon juice until smooth. Whisk in the olive oil, honey, chives, ½ teaspoon salt, and ½ teaspoon pepper until blended. Taste and season with more salt and pepper, if desired. The dressing will keep in an airtight container in the refrigerator for up to 1 week.

CREAMY AVOCADO DRESSING

■ MAKES ABOUT 1 CUP   Hearty and packed with healthy ingredients, this dressing has a good dose of lemon juice to help the avocado maintain its brilliant green color. It may taste pretty lemony on its own, but when it's tossed in a salad, the flavors balance well. Since the dressing is so creamy, delicate lettuces have trouble standing up to it, so opt instead for heftier greens and vegetables. My ideal pairing for this dressing is a mix of chopped romaine, jicama, charred corn, cherry tomatoes, black beans, and cilantro. Keep it vegetarian or add leftover meat—both make for a satisfying main-course salad thanks to the healthful fats and fiber in the avocado.

1 ripe avocado, pitted, peeled, and coarsely chopped

2 tablespoons fresh lemon juice (from about 1 lemon)

½ teaspoon honey

¼ teaspoon ground coriander

Kosher salt

¼ cup avocado oil or mild extra-virgin olive oil

1 tablespoon crème fraîche

In a small food processor or blender, combine the avocado, lemon juice, honey, coriander, and ¼ teaspoon salt. Process the mixture until well blended. With the motor running, drizzle in the avocado oil and continue to process until all the oil is incorporated. Add the crème fraîche and blend until incorporated. Taste and season with more salt as desired.

GRILLED PEACHES

WITH CORIANDER, OPAL BASIL, AND BURRATA

■ SERVES 4   Sometimes the simplest dishes are the most delicious. My husband and I went to the restaurant Nopi in London after I had finished competing at the London Olympics and loved an appetizer there that inspired this one. Use the very best of each ingredient and they will shine. This is a great appetizer to make when peaches are at their peak. Opal basil is a dark purple color and has a more savory taste than regular basil, but if you can't find it, the regular kind will work just fine.

If you happen to grow your own cilantro, let some of it go to seed and use the green seeds in this dish. Otherwise, store-bought dried coriander seeds are just fine. Both add a wonderful herbaceous note to this dish.

1 teaspoon coriander seeds

8 ounces burrata cheese

2 tablespoons very thinly sliced fresh opal basil leaves

2 peaches, unpeeled, pitted and cut into quarters

Extra-virgin olive oil

Maldon sea salt

1. In a dry skillet, toast the coriander seeds over medium heat until they are lightly browned and fragrant, 2 to 3 minutes. Transfer the seeds to a mortar and pestle, and grind until you have a coarse powder. (Alternatively, grind them in a spice grinder.)

2. In the center of each of four serving plates, place one quarter of the burrata. Sprinkle the ground coriander evenly over each piece of burrata and around the edges of each plate. Sprinkle the basil evenly around each burrata.

3. Heat a grill pan over medium-high heat (or preheat a grill to medium-high). Place the peaches on the grill, flesh-side down, and grill until they are lightly charred and easily pull away from the pan, 3 to 5 minutes. Flip the peaches over and grill (still flesh-side down) until they are warmed through, 2 to 3 more minutes. Place 2 peach quarters on each plate, on top of the burrata.

4. To finish, drizzle with the olive oil and sprinkle with a pinch of sea salt. Serve immediately.

CHARRED GREEN BEAN SALAD

WITH PEANUTS AND FRIED SHALLOTS

■ **SERVES 2 TO 4**   One of the vegetables that I always plant in my garden is green beans. In the summer, when they are in their prime and overflowing in my kitchen, I get to be creative with how I cook them. My simplest go-to is to char them in a cast-iron skillet, seasoning them with some soy sauce as they cook. When I want something with a bit more going on, I make this salad, which is inspired by a dish I encountered in a Thai restaurant in Dubai. They served their version with chicken breast and grapefruit segments, which would be nice to add if you want to make it more substantial. I love the vibrant Southeast Asian flavors, as well as the texture of the fried shallots and roasted peanuts.

1 to 2 cups vegetable oil, for frying

1 large shallot, thinly sliced into rounds

Kosher salt

¼ cup fresh lime juice (from about 2 limes)

1 teaspoon fish sauce, plus more for serving

1 tablespoon palm sugar or light brown sugar

1 fresh Thai chile, seeded and finely chopped

¼ cup extra-virgin olive oil

1 pound green beans, trimmed and cut into 3-inch lengths

2 teaspoons soy sauce or tamari

¼ cup roasted peanuts, coarsely chopped

1. Line a wire rack with several layers of paper towels.

2. In a medium saucepan, heat the vegetable oil over high heat. To test if the oil is ready to fry, insert the handle of a wooden spoon into the oil; if the oil bubbles up, you're ready to go. Add the sliced shallots to the hot oil and fry, stirring occasionally, until they turn golden brown, 3 to 5 minutes. Using a spider or a slotted spoon, transfer the shallots to the paper towels. Season them immediately with ⅛ teaspoon salt.

3. In a large bowl, prepare the vinaigrette by whisking together the lime juice, fish sauce, palm sugar, and chile. While whisking constantly, slowly drizzle in the olive oil and continue to whisk until emulsified.

4. Heat a large skillet, preferably cast-iron, over medium-high heat. When the skillet is hot, add the beans to the dry skillet and cook, stirring, until they are charred and slightly wilted, 5 to 8 minutes. Add the soy sauce and quickly toss the wilted beans. (Work quickly, because the soy sauce will evaporate almost immediately.)

5. Transfer the beans to the bowl of vinaigrette, add the chopped peanuts, and toss well. Arrange the bean salad on a serving dish. Just before serving, scatter the fried shallots over the beans. Serve with more fish sauce on the side.

Charred Green Bean Salad
with Peanuts and Fried Shallots

ZUCCHINI, CALABRIAN CHILE, AND MINT SALAD

■ **SERVES 4** The combination of Calabrian chiles and mint is a classic southern Italian flavor profile that I absolutely love. Calabrian chiles have a fruity heat that is unlike any other chile pepper. I often mix these peppers and chopped mint with canned tuna in olive oil for an easy tuna salad. To take these flavors in a vegetarian direction here, I combine them with zucchini, toasted pine nuts, and tomatoes for a versatile summer salad that's delicious warm, cold, or at room temperature.

1½ pounds zucchini, cut lengthwise into quarters, then cut into 1-inch chunks

3 tablespoons extra-virgin olive oil

Kosher salt

3 jarred Calabrian chiles with seeds, minced (about 1 tablespoon; see Note)

1 cup cherry tomatoes, halved or quartered, depending on their size

¼ cup finely chopped fresh mint leaves

⅓ cup pine nuts, toasted (see Note, page 43)

Freshly ground black pepper

1. Preheat the oven to 450°F.

2. On a baking sheet, toss the zucchini with 1 tablespoon of the olive oil and ½ teaspoon salt. Spread the zucchini out in an even layer. Roast, stirring once, until it is browned in parts and cooked through, about 15 minutes.

3. Meanwhile, in a large bowl, combine the remaining 2 tablespoons olive oil, the Calabrian chiles, tomatoes, mint, pine nuts, and ⅛ teaspoon salt. Toss well. Add the hot roasted zucchini and ¼ teaspoon pepper, and toss to combine. Taste and season with more salt and pepper as desired. Serve immediately, or let cool and then serve.

CALABRIAN CHILES Fresh Calabrian chiles can be hard to find. Look for jarred chiles packed in olive oil in the international aisle or canned vegetable aisle of your grocery store. These jarred versions are often seasoned with salt and pepper, so it is important to taste this dish and adjust as necessary. If you can't find Calabrian chiles, a mild to medium-spicy jarred chile packed in oil would work.

CHARRED CORN AND TOMATO SALAD

■ SERVES 4   Sweet summer corn is definitely one of the things I look forward to every year. While I love eating corn straight off the cob, I can't stand the way it gets stuck in my teeth! For this recipe, I cut the kernels off the cob before charring them in a very hot cast-iron skillet. The tomatoes and basil are also essential summery flavors, and the ricotta melts into a creamy sort of sauce that's irresistible. Plus, the best part: no flossing required.

3 ears sweet corn, shucked, kernels sliced off the cobs (about 2¼ cups)

2 tablespoons extra-virgin olive oil

1½ teaspoons honey

1 serrano chile, seeded and finely chopped (optional)

¼ cup ricotta cheese

1 pint cherry tomatoes, halved or quartered, depending on their size

2 scallions, thinly sliced

½ cup thinly sliced fresh basil leaves

Kosher salt and freshly ground black pepper

Heat a large skillet, preferably cast-iron, over medium-high heat. When the skillet is hot, add the corn to the dry skillet and cook, stirring occasionally, until it is charred in parts, about 7 minutes. Reduce the heat to medium and add the olive oil, honey, and serrano, if using. Stir well, cook for 30 seconds, and then remove the pan from the heat. Add the ricotta, tomatoes, scallions, basil, ½ teaspoon salt, and ½ teaspoon pepper. Toss until the ricotta is melted. Taste and season with more salt and pepper as desired.

LENTIL CAPRESE

■ SERVES 4 TO 6   I haven't met a person who doesn't love a caprese salad. Here I've taken the classic combination of fresh mozzarella, tomatoes, and basil and added lentils, which contribute a ton of fiber and plant-based protein, thus turning the dish into a well-rounded meal. You can even scoop it over arugula or a spring lettuce mix to make a bigger salad. As the salad sits, the flavors develop and meld, making this the perfect meal to pack for a picnic, the office, or a flight.

1 cup Umbrian lentils (see Note) or regular brown lentils, rinsed and picked over

4 garlic cloves

1 bay leaf

Kosher salt

⅓ cup extra-virgin olive oil

8 ounces fresh mozzarella cheese, cut into ½-inch cubes

1 pint cherry tomatoes, halved or quartered, depending on their size

½ cup thinly sliced fresh basil leaves

Freshly ground black pepper

1. In a medium saucepan, combine the lentils and 3 cups water. Smash 2 of the garlic cloves and add them to the pot along with the bay leaf. Bring the water to a rapid boil over high heat, then reduce the heat to medium-low. Simmer the lentils until they are tender and cooked through, 20 minutes.

2. Meanwhile, finely mince the remaining 2 cloves of garlic. Sprinkle ¼ teaspoon salt over the garlic and use the side of a chef's knife to mash the garlic into a paste. Put the garlic paste in a medium bowl, add the olive oil, and stir well. Add the mozzarella, tomatoes, basil, and ¼ teaspoon pepper and toss well. Let the mixture sit at room temperature until the lentils are ready.

3. Drain the lentils, and discard the garlic cloves and bay leaf. Stir in ¼ teaspoon salt.

4. Add the cooked lentils to the tomato mixture and toss to combine. Taste and season with salt and pepper as desired.

UMBRIAN LENTILS   Umbrian lentils are smaller than the traditional brown lentils and have fantastic flavor. You can purchase them at Italian specialty stores or well-stocked grocery stores.

SHREDDED BRUSSELS SPROUTS AND KALE SALAD

WITH POMEGRANATE AND CRANBERRIES

SPICED NUTS

1 cup raw pecan halves

1 tablespoon coconut oil

1 tablespoon sugar

¼ teaspoon ground cinnamon

Freshly ground black pepper

⅛ teaspoon cayenne pepper, or to taste

Kosher salt

DRESSING

2 tablespoons extra-virgin olive oil

2 tablespoons raw apple cider vinegar

1 tablespoon honey

1 tablespoon whole-grain mustard

Kosher salt and freshly ground black pepper

SALAD

8 ounces Tuscan kale, ribs removed, leaves cut into ¼-inch-wide ribbons

8 ounces Brussels sprouts, trimmed, cut in half lengthwise, and very thinly sliced

1 cup pomegranate seeds

½ cup dried cranberries

■ SERVES 4 TO 6   This hearty fall salad is one of my go-tos for taking on long plane flights because the Brussels sprouts and kale hold up wonderfully in the dressing—just ignore the jealous passengers around you! It's versatile, too, so swap out the pomegranate seeds and dried cranberries for other fruits, like chopped fresh apple, dried cherries, chopped fresh mango, or sliced persimmon—and try almonds, pistachios, or pumpkin seeds instead of the pecans.

One of the reasons kale has gotten so much good press over the past several years is because it truly is a superfood. It's loaded with vitamins A, C, and K, iron, calcium, and fiber. The fats from the nuts and the olive oil also help you absorb the fat-soluble nutrients (vitamins A and K).

1. **Prepare the spiced nuts**   Line a rimmed baking sheet with parchment paper and set it aside. Set a large cast-iron skillet over medium-low heat. Add the pecans to the dry skillet and toast, stirring them occasionally, until they are fragrant and lightly browned, 5 to 7 minutes. Push the pecans to one side of the pan, and on the other side add 2 tablespoons water, the coconut oil, sugar, cinnamon, ¼ teaspoon black pepper, and the cayenne. Be careful, as the water will bubble up quickly. Cook, stirring constantly to make sure the sugar does not burn, until all the liquid has cooked off and the nuts are well coated with the coconut oil and spices, 1 to 2 minutes. Pour the nuts onto the prepared baking sheet, sprinkle with ¼ teaspoon salt, and let cool. Coarsely chop the cooled nuts.

••• recipe continues •••

2. **Make the dressing**   In a small jar, combine the olive oil, vinegar, honey, mustard, ¼ teaspoon salt, and ¼ teaspoon black pepper. Cover and shake vigorously until the dressing is well blended.

3. **Make the salad**   Combine the kale, Brussels sprouts, pomegranate seeds, and cranberries in a large bowl. Pour the dressing over the salad and toss well. This salad will keep in an airtight container in the refrigerator for up to 24 hours. Just before serving, toss in the spiced pecans.

BEETS WITH ALMONDS

AND ORANGE-SCENTED RICOTTA

■ SERVES 6 TO 8 Beets are nutritional powerhouses—packed with phytonutrients, fiber, iron, and much more—though they are often overlooked, or avoided, for their earthy flavor. There are many ways to prepare this humble root vegetable, but this may be one of the easiest. The vinegar and spices season the beets as they cook, perfuming them and toning down their earthiness. The citrus-flavored ricotta is fresh, creamy, and perfectly salty, while the almonds add a nice touch of crunch. Enjoy this composed salad warm, at room temperature, or cold. And if you have beautiful mircrogreens from the market, toss a tandful on top!

½ cup natural whole (raw) almonds

1 orange

½ cup raw apple cider vinegar

Kosher salt

1 teaspoon fennel seeds

10 whole black peppercorns

1½ pounds beets, trimmed, peeled, and cut into 1-inch cubes

¾ cup ricotta cheese

Freshly ground black pepper

2 tablespoons extra-virgin olive oil

1. Preheat the oven to 350°F.

2. Scatter the almonds on a rimmed baking sheet and toast them in the oven until they are fragrant and lightly browned, about 8 minutes. Let the almonds cool slightly and then coarsely chop them. Set them aside.

3. Using a vegetable peeler, peel 3 strips of the orange zest, avoiding the white pith, that are about 1 inch wide and 4 inches long. Set the strips aside. Using a Microplane, finely grate the remaining orange zest and set it aside. Reserve the zested orange.

4. In a large pot, combine the 3 strips of orange zest, the apple cider vinegar, 1½ teaspoons salt, the fennel seeds, peppercorns, and 2 cups water. Set a steamer basket in the pot. The liquid should reach the bottom of the basket but not above it; add another cup of water if needed. Put the beets in the steamer basket. Set the pot over medium-low to medium heat and cover it; bring the liquid to a simmer. Cook until the beets are tender, 30 to 40 minutes.

5. Meanwhile, in a small bowl, combine the grated orange zest, ricotta, ¼ teaspoon salt, and ¼ teaspoon pepper. Stir well and refrigerate until the beets are ready.

6. Into a large bowl, squeeze 2 tablespoons juice from the zested orange. Whisk vigorously while drizzling in the olive oil. Add ¼ teaspoon salt and ¼ teaspoon pepper.

7. Toss the hot cooked beets in the bowl of vinaigrette until they are well coated. Transfer the beets to a serving platter and dollop the ricotta over them. Sprinkle the chopped almonds on top and serve right away or allow to cool and serve at room temperature.

HOMEMADE CHICKEN STOCK

■ **MAKES 2 QUARTS** Chicken stock is another item, along with salad dressing, that I refuse to buy at the grocery store. When I first started cooking, I didn't understand why anyone would ever make their own chicken stock; it's time-consuming and there are plenty of decent prepared versions out there. And while I still think that there are passable commercial stocks, nothing compares to a long-simmered homemade stock. The flavor is much cleaner and the liquid has more body than its store-bought counterpart. Plus, you can make it with scraps that you save in your freezer, and you can prepare it in a stockpot, pressure cooker, or slow cooker. I prefer to use a slow cooker because I don't have to monitor it during the cooking time.

This recipe is merely an outline for a basic chicken stock. Feel free to change it up according to what you have on hand. While I will often make stock with bones that haven't been cooked yet, I also like to get a "second life" out of leftover bones from a cooked chicken—there's still a lot of great flavor in those bones. I keep a gallon-size plastic zip-top bag in the freezer and fill it with chicken bones from other recipes (Roasted Chicken Legs with Kabocha Squash, on page 184, for instance), and when that bag is filled, I bust out the slow cooker and make this stock.

DON'T HAVE A SLOW COOKER? NOT TO WORRY.

This stock can be made on the stove the traditional way. Put the chicken bones and pieces in a large stockpot and cover them with 12 cups water. Bring it to a boil over high heat. Boil for a few minutes, then reduce the heat to the lowest setting. Use a large spoon to skim off any foam that forms; discard the foam.

At this point, it is very important to not allow the mixture to return to a boil, which would result in a cloudy stock. Add all the remaining ingredients and let the mixture barely simmer for at least 3 hours; you can certainly cook it longer if you have the time.

Set a cheesecloth-lined sieve over a large bowl. Using a ladle, pour the liquid through the sieve until all the solids have been strained out of the stock; discard the solids. Taste and season with salt as desired.

---

1 gallon plastic zip-top bag full of chicken bones and pieces (about 2 carcasses)

1 large onion, chopped

1 leek, cut in half lengthwise and chopped

2 carrots, peeled and chopped

2 celery stalks, chopped

1 head of garlic, cut in half crosswise (papery skin left on)

4 sprigs fresh parsley

4 sprigs fresh thyme

1 bay leaf (fresh or dried)

1 to 2 teaspoons whole black peppercorns

Kosher salt

1. In a large slow cooker, combine the chicken bones, onion, leek, carrots, celery, garlic, parsley, thyme, bay leaf, peppercorns, and 1 teaspoon salt. Cover with water, up to about 2 inches below the rim of the slow cooker. Cover and cook on Low for at least 8 hours and up to 24 hours.

2. Set a cheesecloth-lined sieve over a large bowl. Using a ladle, pour the liquid through the sieve until all the solids have been strained out of the stock; discard the solids. Taste and season the stock with salt as desired. At this point, you can use the stock right away or let it cool to room temperature (see Note) and save it for a later use. The stock will keep in the fridge for up to 3 days or in the freezer for up to 6 months.

VERY IMPORTANT FOOD SAFETY NOTE   Never put hot stock directly into the fridge or freezer. The center of the stock will not cool quickly enough, making it vulnerable to bacteria growth. Let it cool completely to room temperature first. Or, if you need to save time, there are ways to cool the stock more quickly: If it is cold outside, I'll place the bowl of stock outside, cover it with cheesecloth, and let it cool. I'll give it a stir every 15 minutes or so until it reaches room temperature, then transfer it to a storage container and keep it in the fridge or freezer. Or you can make an ice bath by nestling a large bowl of the stock in a larger bowl of ice water. Stir occasionally until the stock has cooled to room temperature, then store.

BROWN CHICKEN STOCK   Brown chicken stock has a deeper, more roasted flavor than basic stock. Which version you make is a matter of preference—for heartier recipes, you may prefer the brown stock. To make it, toss the chicken bones with 1 tablespoon vegetable oil and arrange them on an aluminum foil–lined baking sheet. Roast in a 450°F oven until the bones are deeply browned, 30 to 40 minutes. Then transfer the bones to the slow cooker and proceed with the recipe.

SMOKY GAZPACHO

■ SERVES 4 Gazpacho is the quintessential soup of summer. I have a hard time passing it up whenever it's on the menu at a restaurant, and making it at home couldn't be simpler. It's a refreshing and simple way to use up plenty of those beautiful heirloom tomatoes that you see at the farmer's markets at the peak of summer. My version adds a touch of smoke by first smoking the tomatoes and peppers on a grill. If you've never used your grill as a smoker, you're in for a pleasant surprise—it's an easy technique for producing a nice smoky flavor.

1 cup wood chips, for smoking

2½ pounds heirloom tomatoes, cored and halved

1 pound red bell peppers, halved, stemmed, and seeded

1 large cucumber, peeled, seeded, and coarsely chopped

3 scallions, white parts only, coarsely chopped

1 cup cubed day-old baguette

1 garlic clove (see Note)

1 serrano chile, seeded and coarsely chopped

1 teaspoon red wine vinegar

Kosher salt and freshly ground black pepper

½ cup extra-virgin olive oil

Diced avocado, for garnish (optional)

Finely chopped fresh cilantro, for garnish (optional)

1. Place the wood chips in a medium bowl, cover them with a few inches of water, and let them soak for at least 30 minutes.

2. Heat a charcoal grill to medium-low heat (see Note). Once the grill is properly heated, drain the wood chips and scatter them among the coals. Place the grate on the grill. Arrange the tomatoes and bell peppers on the grill, cut-side up. Cover the grill and smoke until the vegetables are softened and lightly charred, 10 to 15 minutes. Transfer the vegetables to a large bowl and cover it with plastic wrap. Let it sit for about 10 minutes or until the vegetables are cool enough to handle.

3. Using your hands, remove and discard the skins from the tomatoes and peppers. Remove and discard the seeds from the tomatoes. (Don't worry about removing every last seed and bit of skin; leaving a few will be fine.) Reserve any juices that collect in the bowl.

4. Put the tomatoes, peppers, and any reserved juices in a blender and puree until smooth. Add the cucumber, scallions, bread, garlic, chile, vinegar, ¼ teaspoon salt, and ¼ teaspoon black pepper to the blender. Blend until smooth. Turn the blender on low and, with the motor running, gradually add the olive oil. Taste and season with

salt and black pepper as desired. Transfer the soup to an airtight container and refrigerate it for at least 1 hour before serving. (The gazpacho will keep in the refrigerator for up to 3 days.)

5. When ready to serve, garnish the soup with avocado and cilantro, if desired.

GAS GRILL   You can also smoke using a gas grill, though it takes a bit longer and the results lack that flavor that comes from the charcoal. Some gas grills have a smoker box, but if yours doesn't, put the drained soaked wood chips in a disposable aluminum container and, before preheating the grill, set the container directly on the heat source (under the grates). Preheat the grill as instructed in the recipe. Smoke the veggies for about 30 minutes.

RAW GARLIC   When using raw garlic in a dish, make sure to remove the green shoot, if there is one in the center, as it can impart a bitter, "hot" flavor. If you're cooking the garlic, don't bother—I've never noticed a difference in taste.

Smoky Gazpacho

RESTORATIVE GARLIC SOUP

■ **MAKES 3½ CUPS** When I was competing on *Dancing with the Stars,* my makeup artist, Melanie Mills, gave me this recipe one day when I was feeling under the weather. Now, I turn to this soup whenever I need a little pick-me-up. No matter how much we try to avoid it, everyone gets run-down from time to time, and we often forget that many foods have powerful medicinal qualities. Chicken soup is widely revered for its healing capabilities; it hydrates and provides minerals, fat, and protein in a form that's easy to eat and digest when you can't fathom having an appetite. This soup has a base of chicken stock, and adding lots of garlic—which has been used in holistic medicine for generations—boosts its healing properties while lending the soup wonderful flavor. The garlicky taste is smooth and rounded—not sharp and pungent, as you would get with raw garlic. You'll be happily surprised by how cozy and comforting a bowl of this soup is on a sick day!

2 tablespoons unsalted butter

25 garlic cloves,
coarsely chopped

1 quart chicken stock, homemade
(see page 68) or store-bought

⅛ teaspoon freshly grated
nutmeg, or more to taste

Kosher salt and freshly
ground black pepper

2 large egg yolks

¼ cup heavy cream

Fresh chives, minced,
for garnish (optional)

1. In a medium pot, melt the butter over medium heat. When the butter is melted and foamy, add the garlic. Cook, stirring occasionally, until the garlic is soft and golden, about 3 minutes. Add the chicken stock and season with the nutmeg and salt and pepper to taste. Bring the mixture to a boil, stirring occasionally, then reduce the heat to low and simmer for 5 minutes. Remove the pot from the heat.

2. In a medium bowl, whisk together the egg yolks and heavy cream. While whisking, add ¼ cup of the garlic broth to the egg mixture (this will bring the temperature of the egg yolks up slowly so they don't scramble). Pour the yolk mixture and the remaining garlic broth into a blender and blend until smooth. (You can also use an immersion blender, but a regular blender creates a soothing silkiness.)

3. Taste and season with salt and pepper as desired. Garnish with the chives, if desired, and serve hot.

PEELING GARLIC   Here's a simple technique for peeling large amounts of garlic: Pull the stem off the head of garlic and remove the loose outer skins. Place the head on your cutting board, flat-side down, and use the heel of your hand to crush it into separate cloves. Trim the brown roots off the cloves, and then use the side of a chef's knife to smash the cloves. They should now separate easily from the papery skin.

FILIPINO HAM HOCK SOUP

■ SERVES 8 TO 10 Growing up as a swimmer in Northern California, I got used to being chilled to the bone during the winter and early spring months. The rainfall seemed never-ending, and the pool water was never warm enough. Because of this, I grew to love soup in any form because a bowl of warm liquid always managed to heat me through and through. This simple, comforting soup is my great-grandma's version of the traditional *calandracas* of the Philippines and is a perfect example of humble ingredients transformed into something delicious.

2 ham hocks

1 large boneless, skinless chicken breast

1 tablespoon grapeseed oil or other high-heat neutral oil (see page 20)

3 garlic cloves, minced

1 large onion, chopped (about 2 cups)

1 cup chopped celery (about 3 stalks)

2 pieces chorizo de Bilbao (see Note) or other semi-cured chorizo, chopped

1½ cups chopped peeled potatoes (any type is fine)

1 cup drained canned chickpeas

Kosher salt and freshly ground black pepper

8 ounces small shell pasta

1. Put the ham hocks in a large stockpot, add 12 cups water, and bring the water to a boil over medium-high heat. Reduce the heat to medium, partially cover the pot, and simmer for 60 to 90 minutes. Begin to check the meat after an hour; the ham hocks are ready once the meat is falling off the bone.

2. Add the chicken breast to the pot and simmer until it is tender and cooked through, about 7 minutes. Remove from the heat and transfer the ham hocks and chicken to a cutting board. Dice the meats and discard the ham bones and skin.

3. In a medium sauté pan, combine the grapeseed oil and the garlic. Cook over medium heat, stirring, until the garlic is fragrant and golden, 30 seconds. Add the onion and celery and cook, stirring, until they are just beginning to soften, 2 minutes. Transfer this mixture to the pot of stock and add the chorizo, potatoes, and chickpeas. Simmer for 15 minutes over medium-high heat, until the potatoes are cooked through.

4. Season the soup with ⅓ teaspoon salt and ¼ teaspoon pepper, and return the meat to the pot. Bring the mixture back to a simmer, then add the shell pasta. Cook, following the package directions, until the pasta is al dente. Taste and season with more salt and pepper as desired.

CHORIZO DE BILBAO   This spicy, semi-cured pork and beef sausage (well loved in both the Philippines and Spain) may require a trip to an Asian or Spanish grocery store—or feel free to substitute linguiça.

LAZY RAMEN

This recipe starts with regular chicken stock and becomes a simple yet satisfying ramen bowl for when I want to enjoy the dish at home. As always, homemade chicken stock is the best to use, due to its taste and body, but you can definitely use a store-bought stock here. The roasted aromatics, miso paste, kombu, and fish sauce add layers of umami-packed flavor. It's a broth that's great sipped on its own, but you can add any number of items (see How to Build a Ramen Bowl, page 81), including Soy-Marinated Eggs (page 80), to make a satisfying meal.

EASY RAMEN BROTH

2 tablespoons white miso paste

1 tablespoon grapeseed oil or other high-heat neutral oil (see page 20)

1 (3-inch) piece fresh ginger, unpeeled

1 large onion, unpeeled, quartered

8 scallions, cut into 4-inch-long pieces

1 (3 x 4-inch) piece kombu

3 quarts chicken stock, homemade (see page 68) or store-bought

2 or 3 dried bird's eye chiles

1 or 2 star anise pods

1 ounce dried shiitake mushrooms, coarsely chopped

1 tablespoon fish sauce, plus more for seasoning

1 tablespoon mirin, plus more for seasoning

■ MAKES 1½ TO 2 QUARTS   This is by no means an authentic ramen recipe. Traditional ramen broth, such as *tonkotsu*, my favorite style, can take upward of 24 hours to make. The long, intensive process involves a huge amount of various pork bones and copious chopped pork fat. I'd rather leave that one to the professionals and enjoy it in ignorant bliss!

1. Preheat the oven to 350°F.

2. In a small bowl, whisk together the miso paste, grapeseed oil, and a splash of hot water until smooth. On a rimmed baking sheet, toss the miso mixture with the ginger, onion, and scallions. Roast until the vegetables are slightly charred and oozing, 45 to 60 minutes.

3. Meanwhile, rinse the kombu under running water. Put it in a bowl, cover it with water, and let it soak while you bring the chicken stock to a simmer in a large saucepan over high heat. Add the drained kombu to the gently simmering stock, partially cover the pot, and cook to infuse the stock with the flavor of the kombu, 30 minutes. Discard the kombu and remove the pot from the heat.

•••• recipe continues ••••

4. When the vegetables are roasted, add them to the chicken stock along with the dried chiles, star anise, and dried mushrooms. Set the saucepan over high heat, bring the broth to a gentle simmer, and reduce the heat to medium-low. Partially cover the pot and allow the ingredients to infuse the broth for 1 hour. You want the broth to barely simmer.

5. Strain the broth and discard the solids. Add the fish sauce and mirin. Taste and season with more fish sauce and/or mirin as desired. Use immediately or let cool completely and store for later use. The ramen broth will keep in an airtight container in the refrigerator for up to 3 days or in the freezer for up to 6 months.

SOY-MARINATED EGGS

1 cup soy sauce or tamari

½ cup mirin

½ cup sake

2 tablespoons sugar

2 garlic cloves, peeled and smashed with the side of a knife

1 (1-inch) piece fresh ginger, unpeeled, sliced into coins (about the thickness of a nickel)

6 large eggs, at room temperature

■ MAKES 6 EGGS A classic addition to a ramen bowl or bento box, *shoyu tamago* are soft-boiled eggs that are marinated in a soy-based liquid to produce a salty, sweet, creamy bite that's just irresistible.

1. Prepare the marinade by combining 1 cup water, the soy sauce, mirin, sake, sugar, garlic, and ginger in a small saucepan. Set the pan over high heat and bring the mixture to a rolling boil. Boil for 1 minute, making sure that the sugar dissolves, then remove the pan from the heat. Let the marinade cool to room temperature (you will have 3 cups).

2. Meanwhile, prepare the eggs: Bring a medium pot of water to a boil. Prepare a bowl of ice water that's larger than you think you'll need, and set it beside the pot. (Stopping the eggs from overcooking is a very important step.) Once the water is boiling gently, carefully place the eggs in the water and cook for 7 minutes for runny eggs, 8 minutes for thicker yolks. Be sure to maintain a gentle simmer. Immediately transfer the eggs to the ice water. Let them cool for at least 5 minutes before peeling them.

Ramen is both delicious and fun to eat because of all the tasty ingredients swimming in the bowl. Here are some of my favorite additions to mix and match for a filling meal.

Fresh or dried Chinese egg noodles, cooked

Soy-Marinated Eggs (opposite)

Leftover meat, thinly sliced

Finely sliced scallions

Baby mustard greens

Baby kale

Spinach

Chard greens, lightly steamed

Bamboo shoots

Enoki mushrooms

Grated fresh ginger

Grated garlic

Freshly sprouted greens

Easy Ramen Broth (page 78)

Shichimi togarashi

- Once you have all your ingredients ready to go, building a ramen bowl couldn't be simpler. If you have a ramen bowl, that's great. Otherwise use the largest, deepest soup bowl you have.

- The proportions of your ramen fillings are totally up to you, but I aim for about 1 cup noodles; 1 soy-marinated egg, halved; ¼ cup leftover meat; and 1 to 2 cups vegetables.

- Place your cooked noodles in a mound in the center of your bowl. Place the vegetables on one side of the noodle mound, the meat nestled next to the vegetables, and the soy-marinated egg halves next to the veggies. Top the ingredients with 2 cups or more of hot ramen broth.

- If you like spice, as I do, I sprinkle some *shichimi togarashi* (Japanese 7-spice blend) on top just before serving. Serve immediately.

3. Put the peeled eggs in a container that will just barely hold the eggs and the marinade. Once the marinade is at room temperature, pour it over the eggs and cover the container. Let the eggs marinate for at least 4 hours and up to overnight; then discard the marinade. The marinated eggs will keep in an airtight container in the refrigerator for up to 3 days.

VEGETABLES

MISO-ROASTED SWEET POTATOES

■ SERVES 4 TO 6 Miso paste is one of my favorite ingredients. Its savory, salty, sweet characteristics add a ton of flavor to a variety of dishes beyond the ubiquitous miso soup. I particularly love how miso contrasts so well with the slight sweetness and earthiness of sweet potatoes. This dish is fantastic served simply as a side to grilled meats, though I also love pairing the cooled potatoes with peppery wild arugula for a colorful salad or tossing them into a grain bowl.

2 tablespoons coconut oil

1 teaspoon ground ginger

½ teaspoon cayenne pepper

3 pounds sweet potatoes, peeled and cut into 1-inch cubes

Kosher salt

¼ cup white miso paste

2 tablespoons maple syrup

1 tablespoon white sesame seeds, lightly toasted (see Note, page 43)

1. Preheat the oven to 450°F.

2. If the coconut oil is solid, heat it up so that it becomes liquid; about 20 seconds in the microwave should do the trick. In a small bowl, combine the coconut oil, ginger, and cayenne. Put the sweet potatoes on a rimmed baking sheet, drizzle with the oil mixture, and toss to coat them evenly. Spread the sweet potatoes out in a single layer. Sprinkle with ⅛ teaspoon salt. Roast until partially cooked, about 30 minutes, stirring once after 15 minutes.

3. Meanwhile, in a small bowl, combine the miso paste and maple syrup.

4. Remove the sweet potatoes from the oven, drizzle the miso mixture over them, and toss until they are evenly coated. Return the baking sheet to the oven and roast until the sweet potatoes are fully cooked and browned in places, about 10 minutes.

5. Sprinkle the white sesame seeds over the sweet potatoes and serve.

EVERYTHING-BUT-THE-KITCHEN-SINK STIR-FRY

■ SERVES 2 Growing up, we ate stir-fry quite often. Fast, easy to prepare, and endlessly versatile, it's a great way to clean out the fridge and end up with a satisfying meal. I like to pack in the veggies as much as possible, round out the meal with a bit of protein, and garnish it with herbs, hot sauce, and/or sliced scallions. Think of this recipe as a template and use the chart on the opposite page as inspiration. The key when stir-frying is to get everything ready before you start cooking; so line all your ingredients up, get your wok or pan very hot, and you'll have dinner ready in no time.

6 to 8 ounces protein

Cooking oil

1 tablespoon aromatics

1 cup (or more) vegetables

1 cup cooked grain or noodles

¼ cup Stir-Fry Sauce (see page 88), or soy sauce or fish sauce to taste

Garnishes

1. Heat a large wok or skillet over medium-high heat. Using paper towels, pat the **protein** of your choice very dry. To the hot pan, add 1 tablespoon **cooking oil** and the protein, and cook, stirring, until cooked through. Add more oil if necessary. Transfer the protein to a plate.

2. To the hot pan, add 1 to 2 tablespoons cooking oil and the **aromatics** of your choice. Stir-fry for 30 seconds. Add the toughest **vegetables** you've chosen and stir-fry for 1 to 2 minutes. Continue adding the vegetables in order of toughness, from toughest to softest. (You'll want at least 1 cup vegetables total—the more, the better!) Cook, stirring, until the vegetables reach your desired doneness.

3. Return the cooked protein to the pan and add the **cooked grain or noodles** and **Stir-Fry Sauce** or soy sauce or fish sauce. Toss to combine. Add more sauce if necessary. Cook, stirring, until heated through. Serve immediately with the **garnishes** of your choice.

STIR-FRY INGREDIENTS

I've listed some examples of what you can stir-fry here,
but you are limited only by your imagination!

COOKING OIL

Peanut oil
Grapeseed oil
Other high-heat neutral oil (see page 20)

PROTEIN

Chicken | cut into 1-inch cubes, seasoned with salt and pepper

Shrimp | peeled and deveined, seasoned with salt and pepper

Beef | cut into 1-inch cubes, seasoned with salt and pepper

Tofu | cut into 1-inch cubes, dried with paper towels

Ground meats | seasoned with salt and pepper

AROMATICS
(any combination of)

Garlic | minced
Fresh ginger | peeled and minced
Fresh chiles | minced

VEGETABLES
(any combination of)

Onions | chopped

Bell peppers | cored, seeded, and chopped

Carrots | peeled and cut into matchsticks

Broccoli | cut into small florets

Zucchini | chopped

Mushrooms | stemmed and thinly sliced

Eggplant | chopped

Snap peas | cut into bite-size pieces

Green beans | cut into bite-size pieces

Asparagus | cut into bite-size pieces

Kale | ribs removed, leaves thinly sliced

Cabbage | shredded

Swiss chard | stems chopped (added earlier with the harder veggies), leaves thinly sliced

Bok choy | thinly sliced

Peas | shelled

COOKED GRAIN or NOODLES

Brown or white rice
Farro
Barley
Quinoa

Chinese egg noodles | tossed with a splash of sesame oil

Rice stick noodles | soaked and drained, tossed with a splash of oil of your choice

SAUCE

Stir-Fry Sauce (see page 88)
Soy sauce or tamari
Fish sauce

GARNISHES

Scallions | thinly sliced
Chile paste
Sriracha
Fresh cilantro | coarsely chopped

Fresh basil | coarsely chopped
Fresh parsley | coarsely chopped
Scrambled or fried eggs

Peanuts | coarsely chopped
Sesame seeds | toasted
Furikake seasoning

••• recipe continues •••

STIR-FRY SAUCE

■ MAKES ABOUT 2 CUPS (ABOUT EIGHT ¼-CUP SERVINGS)   What transforms a decent stir-fry into a great one is a really good sauce. I totally get the convenience factor of store-bought stir-fry sauce. If you look at the ingredient labels, however, you'll see that they are filled with all sorts of things that you really don't want to put in your body. Take a few minutes and make this one ahead of time. I promise it will be worth it!

This stir-fry sauce is quite salty, but keep in mind that it will season your veggies, protein, and grains, so a little bit goes a long way. It keeps very well, too, staying fresh in a jar in your fridge for up to a week—or you can transfer it to ice cube trays to store in the freezer for up to 6 months (the sauce won't freeze solid because of the high salt content, but it will still be preserved). I like to make a double batch and employ the freezer option. That way, I can easily whip up a tasty stir-fry whenever the craving strikes.

1 cup chicken stock, homemade (see page 68) or store-bought

2 tablespoons cornstarch

½ cup soy sauce or tamari

⅓ cup dry sherry or rice vinegar

¼ cup mirin

2 tablespoons fish sauce

1 tablespoon toasted sesame oil

1 tablespoon grapeseed oil or other high-heat neutral oil (see page 20)

1 tablespoon grated garlic (from 3 or 4 cloves)

1 tablespoon grated fresh ginger

1 teaspoon crushed red pepper flakes, plus more for seasoning as desired (optional)

1 tablespoon light brown sugar

Freshly ground black pepper

1. In a small bowl, whisk together ¼ cup of the chicken stock and the cornstarch.

2. In a medium bowl, combine the remaining ¾ cup stock, the soy sauce, sherry, mirin, fish sauce, and sesame oil.

3. In a medium saucepan, combine the grapeseed oil, garlic, ginger, and red pepper flakes (if using). Cook over medium-high heat, stirring constantly, until fragrant, 30 seconds. Add the stock-soy mixture and bring to a boil. Reduce the heat to medium-low. Whisk in the cornstarch slurry and return the mixture to a boil. Cook, undisturbed, until thickened, 1 minute, then whisk in the brown sugar and ¼ teaspoon black pepper. Taste and season with more red pepper flakes or ¼ teaspoon black pepper as desired.

CHANGE IT UP   You can change up the basic stir-fry sauce recipe in any number of ways. Try adding one or more of the following:
- orange zest to the stock-soy mixture
- coconut milk or creamy peanut butter just before adding the cornstarch slurry
- grated lemon or lime zest at the end with the black pepper
- ground Sichuan peppercorns with or in place of the black pepper

PARMESAN MASHED CAULIFLOWER

WITH SPICY GREENS AND EGGS

■ SERVES 2 This recipe was born out of laziness. I needed to clean out my fridge and was also looking for something to eat, but it was a rainy January day and I refused to make a trip to the grocery store. Thanks to my garden and hens, I had an abundance of mustard greens and eggs, and I discovered a lonely cauliflower in my crisper drawer. And voilà! This rich, cheesy mash is a great match for the earthy greens, and who doesn't love a dish with fried eggs on top? And it just happens to be both healthy and hearty, too.

1 head cauliflower, cut into florets

2 bunches mustard greens (1½ to 2 pounds), well rinsed (or a mix of other dark greens such as Swiss chard, bok choy, kale, or collards)

Kosher salt

2 tablespoons unsalted butter

¼ cup finely grated Parmesan cheese

Freshly ground black pepper

3 tablespoons grapeseed oil or other high-heat neutral oil (see page 20)

Hefty pinch of crushed red pepper flakes

2 garlic cloves, minced

2 tablespoons aged balsamic vinegar

4 large eggs

Maldon sea salt, for serving

1. Fill a pot with a few inches of water and set a steamer basket in the pot. Place the cauliflower florets in the basket, cover the pot, and set it over medium-high heat. Once steam condenses on the lid, reduce the heat to medium-low and steam until the cauliflower is soft, 15 minutes.

2. Meanwhile, remove the stems from the leaves of the mustard greens and finely chop the stems. Coarsely chop the leaves.

3. Remove the cauliflower from the steamer, reserving ¼ cup of the steaming liquid, and dump out the rest of the liquid (reserve the empty pot). When the cauliflower is cool enough to handle, transfer it to a food processor. Pulse a few times, scraping the sides of the bowl if necessary. Add 1 teaspoon kosher salt and process until you have a smooth puree. Add the butter and Parmesan, and process until incorporated. Taste and season with kosher salt and black pepper as desired. Cover and set aside.

4. Set the reserved pot over medium-high heat and add 1 tablespoon of the grapeseed oil, the red pepper flakes, a small pinch of kosher salt, and the stems of the mustard greens. Cook, stirring, until the stems are tender, 5 to 7 minutes. Add the garlic and cook, stirring, until fragrant, 30 seconds. Add the mustard leaves and the reserved ¼ cup steaming water. Cook, stirring, until the leaves are tender and the liquid has evaporated, about 5 minutes. Remove the pot from the heat and stir in the vinegar. Taste and season with kosher salt and black pepper as desired.

5. Spoon the mashed cauliflower into two serving bowls. Divide the greens between the bowls. Keep the bowls hot while you cook the eggs.

6. Heat a large cast-iron or nonstick skillet over medium-high heat. Crack one of the eggs into a small bowl, and have the other 3 eggs close by. When the pan is hot, add the remaining 2 tablespoons grapeseed oil and slide the egg into the pan. Quickly crack another egg into the bowl, slide it into the pan, and repeat with the remaining eggs (or work in batches of two if your pan is too small to hold all four, using 1 tablespoon grapeseed oil per batch; try to keep the eggs separate to maximize the crispy edges). The whites will immediately bubble up. Do not touch! Cook until the whites are fully set and the edges are browned and crispy, about 2 minutes. Using a spatula, transfer the eggs to the bowls of cauliflower mash and greens. Season the eggs with a small pinch each of sea salt and black pepper, and serve immediately.

Parmesan Mashed Cauliflower
with Spicy Greens and Eggs

SPANISH TORTILLA

■ SERVES 8 I have traveled to Barcelona several times for competitions and have loved exploring the city's incredible food scene. My teammates and I would usually head out to a local eatery after the evening session of the competition—around 8 o'clock or so—hoping to grab a meal before an early bedtime, as we all needed to rest for the next day of racing. I will never forget the bewildered looks from our servers when we ordered dinner! We were at least two hours early by the local custom.

It's nearly impossible to enjoy a meal of tapas without ordering tortilla, which is basically a frittata made with olive oil–poached potatoes and onions. I often make this dish when I'm craving an excuse to eat aioli. It's wonderful warm, cold, or at room temperature—and when making this at home, I don't have to eat it at 10 p.m. the way the Barcelonans do.

¾ cup olive oil

1 pound Yukon Gold potatoes, peeled, quartered, and very thinly sliced

1 large onion, thinly sliced (about 2 cups)

Kosher salt and freshly ground black pepper

8 large eggs

Smoked Spanish paprika, for garnish

Classic Aioli (recipe follows), for serving

1. Preheat the oven to 300°F.

2. Heat a large cast-iron skillet over medium-low heat. Add the olive oil, potatoes, onion, 1 teaspoon salt, and 1 teaspoon pepper. Cook, stirring frequently, until the onion is soft but not browned and the potatoes are cooked through, 15 to 20 minutes. Set a colander in a bowl, transfer the mixture to the colander, and let it drain, reserving the oil in the bowl.

3. In a large bowl, vigorously whisk the eggs with ¾ teaspoon salt. Fold in the drained potato mixture.

4. Wipe out the skillet and remove any stuck-on bits. Set the skillet over medium heat. Add 1 tablespoon of the reserved oil and spread the egg-potato mixture in the skillet in an even layer. Cook, undisturbed, for 1 minute, then transfer the skillet to the oven.

••• recipe continues •••

5. Bake until the eggs are barely set and jiggle slightly when you shake the skillet, 15 to 20 minutes. Let the tortilla cool for 5 minutes before transferring it to a large platter. Slice it into wedges, sprinkle them lightly with paprika, and serve each slice with a dollop of aioli.

AS AN APP While Spanish Tortilla is great as a light meal, you can transform it into a lovely appetizer: Instead of cutting the cooked tortilla into wedges, use a small cookie cutter to cut out bite-size portions. Arrange them on a platter and place a tiny dollop of aioli on top of each.

LEFTOVER OIL You can reuse the leftover drained olive oil: Set a coffee filter in a fine-mesh strainer and strain the oil through the filter into a container to remove any solids before cooking with it again.

CLASSIC AIOLI

■ MAKES ABOUT 1 CUP As someone who loves garlic, I will make any excuse to whip up a batch of aioli, which is basically a garlicky mayonnaise. I like to use a mild, buttery, high-quality olive oil; those pungent, peppery ones are too overpowering here. Aioli is delicious as a spread on a sandwich, as a dip for oven-baked sweet potato fries, or dolloped on a slice of Spanish Tortilla (page 94). This is the classic recipe, but you can change up the finishing touches any number of ways: with minced fresh herbs, Calabrian chiles, za'atar, sun-dried tomatoes, or capers—or try roasting the garlic first.

2 or 3 garlic cloves (see Note, page 71)

Kosher salt

1 large egg yolk

1 cup extra-virgin olive oil

1 teaspoon fresh lemon juice

1. Using a mortar and pestle, mash the garlic with ⅛ teaspoon salt until it forms a creamy paste (this will take a couple minutes of vigorous work). Whisk in the egg yolk. While vigorously whisking, start to very slowly drizzle in the olive oil. When the mixture is well emulsified, you can drizzle in the olive oil a little more quickly. Continue to whisk until all the oil is incorporated. Whisk in the lemon juice, taste, and season with salt as desired.

2. Transfer the aioli to a jar with a tight-fitting lid. Press a piece of plastic wrap onto the surface of the aioli to limit its exposure to air, and then secure the lid on the jar. Store the aioli in the refrigerator for up to 1 week, but keep in mind that the garlic flavor will intensify with time.

MORTAR AND PESTLE I absolutely love using a mortar and pestle and prefer to use it whenever I make aioli or any type of herbaceous sauce, and for grinding spices. Though working with a food processor would be quicker and easier, I promise you that the mortar and pestle makes a difference. Food processors chop your ingredients into tiny bits, whereas a mortar and pestle crushes them to extract more juices and oils from the ingredients. The resulting sauces are much creamier and more flavorful. When using a mortar and pestle, first mash the garlic (if the recipe calls for garlic) a few times to get the process started. Then, using a circular motion, grind the garlic into a fine paste before adding the other ingredients. I like to alternate mashing and grinding until I get my desired consistency.

ROASTED EGGPLANT

WITH HERBED LABNEH

■ SERVES 4 TO 6 In high school, I refused to eat sandwiches with deli meat, so my mom took to grilling a bunch of vegetables for dinner and saving the leftovers to make veggie-and-cheese sandwiches for my lunch the next day. Eggplant and red bell peppers were always my favorite grilled vegetables, and I love both to this day. Nowadays, I often roast eggplant instead of grilling it because my charcoal grill takes time to set up, and the results are just as delicious.

The herbed labneh is a lovely complement to the roasted eggplant. I first tasted labneh when I was in Australia for a training camp. There's a large Lebanese population there, and therefore there are some excellent Lebanese restaurants. I remember being pleasantly surprised that the rich cheese-like spread I discovered was really just drained yogurt!

2 pounds eggplant, cut into 1-inch cubes

Kosher salt

3 tablespoons olive oil

1 large garlic clove, minced

1 teaspoon ground Aleppo pepper (see Note, page 100)

Herbed Labneh (recipe follows), for serving

1. In a colander, toss the cubed eggplant with a couple of hefty pinches of salt. Set the colander inside a large bowl and let sit at room temperature for 1 hour (see Note, page 100).

2. Meanwhile, in a small bowl, combine the olive oil, garlic, and Aleppo pepper.

3. Preheat the oven to 400°F.

4. Rinse the eggplant cubes under cold running water and dry them immediately using either a salad spinner or paper towels. Put the eggplant on a rimmed baking sheet, drizzle with the olive oil mixture, sprinkle with a pinch of salt, and toss until evenly coated. Spread the eggplant out in a single layer on the baking sheet. Roast, stirring halfway through, until the eggplant is softened and cooked through, 25 to 30 minutes.

5. Smear a tablespoon or so of herbed labneh on each serving plate, top with the eggplant, and serve hot.

••• recipe continues •••

vegetables

SALTING EGGPLANT If you have the time and patience, salting the eggplants and letting them sit for about an hour is well worthwhile, though this dish will still be great if you need to skip this step. The salting purges the vegetable of bitterness and extra liquid. If you didn't plan ahead or don't have the time, don't worry; just season the eggplant cubes with ½ teaspoon kosher salt when you toss them with the seasoned olive oil.

ALEPPO PEPPER There's nothing quite like the heady warmth of Aleppo pepper, but if you need a substitute, use 4 parts sweet paprika and 1 part cayenne pepper.

HERBED LABNEH

■ MAKES ABOUT 1½ CUPS While some specialty markets sell labneh, I find it easier to make my own, since I usually have yogurt around. I prefer to use full-fat Greek yogurt, but feel free to substitute 2% fat. This herbed labneh would be delicious as part of a mezze platter or with crudités; drizzle high-quality olive oil over the labneh right before serving. Nigella seeds are something I started cooking with only after I grew nigella flowers in my garden. The seeds have a mild onion taste and add a nice texture to the herbed labneh. Look for them in the spice aisle.

2 cups full-fat or 2% Greek yogurt

1 tablespoon minced fresh mint

1 tablespoon minced fresh thyme

1 teaspoon minced fresh oregano

1 teaspoon nigella seeds

Kosher salt

1. Line a fine-mesh strainer with a few layers of cheesecloth, making sure the cheesecloth is large enough to wrap around all the yogurt. Place the yogurt in the cheesecloth, bring the ends of the cheesecloth up around the yogurt, and twist until a tight ball is formed. Secure the ends of the cheesecloth with a rubber band. Trim the ends of the cheesecloth, if desired. Set the yogurt ball in the strainer and set the strainer over a bowl. Refrigerate for at least 12 hours or up to 24 hours.

2. Discard any liquid collected in the bowl and give the cheesecloth a squeeze to extract as much water from the yogurt as you can. Put the strained yogurt in a medium bowl and add the mint, thyme, oregano, nigella seeds, and ¼ teaspoon salt. Using a rubber spatula, stir the mixture until the seasonings are thoroughly combined. The herbed labneh will keep in an airtight container in the refrigerator for up to 3 days.

YOGURT-ROASTED CARROTS

■ SERVES 6 I absolutely love the combination of garam masala, cilantro, and carrots. In this dish, inspired by tandoori chicken, yogurt allows the spices to adhere to the carrots while they roast and creates a wonderful tangy crust. The warming spices complement the roasted carrots in a lovely way, and the fresh cilantro makes it all come alive. These carrots are a fantastic side dish to roasted meats, or you can make a large composed salad by combining them with other vegetables, salads, and grains in one big bowl: Charred Green Bean Salad (page 54), Charred Corn and Tomato Salad (page 60), Beets with Almonds and Orange-Scented Ricotta (page 66), Roasted Eggplant with Herbed Labneh (page 99), and Miso-Roasted Sweet Potatoes (page 84) are great to use, along with cooked quinoa, farro, rice, or other grains, and some fresh greens, too. Wonderful when hot out of the oven, these are also lovely at room temperature, making them a great candidate for a picnic or part of an office lunch.

¾ cup full-fat yogurt (not Greek)

3 tablespoons extra-virgin olive oil

1 tablespoon garam masala

Kosher salt and freshly ground black pepper

1½ pounds carrots, trimmed and scrubbed

1 tablespoon fresh lemon juice, plus more if needed

1 teaspoon honey

2 tablespoons finely chopped fresh cilantro

1. Preheat the oven to 450°F. Line a rimmed baking sheet with parchment paper or aluminum foil.

2. In a large bowl, whisk together ½ cup of the yogurt, 2 tablespoons of the olive oil, the garam masala, ½ teaspoon salt, and ½ teaspoon pepper. Using your hands, toss the carrots in the yogurt mixture, making sure to coat every surface of the carrots. Transfer the carrots to the prepared baking sheet and roast until they are browned in places and cooked through, 25 to 30 minutes.

3. Meanwhile, in a small bowl, whisk together the remaining ¼ cup yogurt, remaining 1 tablespoon olive oil, the lemon juice, honey, and cilantro. The consistency should be like a very thin yogurt. Add more lemon juice, if necessary.

4. Transfer the cooked carrots to a serving platter. Taste and season with more salt as desired. Drizzle the carrots with the yogurt-lemon sauce and serve.

HUMMUS-AVOCADO COLLARD GREEN WRAPS

■ MAKES 4 WRAPS This is a wonderful portable wrap to take to the office, to school, or on a plane. I particularly like taking it with me when I travel because it is nearly impossible to get fresh greens at an airport. If it is wrapped tightly in plastic wrap, you can easily eat this on a plane without the filling spilling out. Just peel the plastic wrap away from one end and keep pulling it off as you take bites.

My Avocado Cilantro Hummus (page 122) or Roasted Piquillo Pepper and Garlic Hummus (page 125) would be wonderful in this wrap, but any hummus will do. Feel free to change up the grains and veggies to suit your preference. This recipe is vegan, but you can certainly add meat or cheese if you like. Search for the biggest collard greens you can find, since their large size will make wrapping much easier.

4 large collard greens (see Note)

1 cup hummus

1 cup cooked quinoa or cooked grain of your choice

Kosher salt and freshly ground black pepper

1 ripe avocado, pitted, peeled, and thinly sliced

1 cup thinly shredded red cabbage

1 large carrot, peeled and finely grated

1 daikon radish, peeled and finely grated

1 cup microgreens or sprouts

1. To prepare the collard greens, trim off and discard the part of the stem that extends past the bottom of each leaf. Fold the leaf in half lengthwise and carefully cut out most of the stem with a sharp knife. The goal is to remove as much of the stem as possible while keeping the leaf intact.

2. Place one collard leaf on a cutting board with the tip of the leaf on your left and the base of the leaf on your right. Spread ¼ cup of the hummus in the center of the leaf, along the stem, leaving a couple of inches of space on the right and left ends of the leaf. Spoon one-quarter of the quinoa next to the hummus, on the side farthest away from you, and season it with salt and pepper. Pile one-quarter of the avocado, cabbage, carrot, daikon, and microgreens on top of the quinoa, leaving a couple of inches of space on the right and left ends of the leaf.

3. To roll the wrap, fold the bottom edge of the leaf (the one closest to you) over the vegetable filling and then tightly fold in the right and left sides the leaf. Roll up the leaf to seal the filling completely (like a burrito). Place it seam-side down on a plate and repeat with the remaining collard leaves and filling.

4. Enjoy immediately, or tightly wrap each one in plastic wrap and take them along with you.

STEAMED COLLARDS   If you prefer not to eat the collard greens raw, you can steam them prior to wrapping: In a pot fitted with a steamer basket, bring an inch of water to a boil. Put the trimmed greens in the basket and steam until they are bright green, 20 to 30 seconds. Let cool and pat dry before using.

Hummus-Avocado
Collard Green Wraps

ZUCCHINI-CARROT FRITTERS

■ MAKES ABOUT 12 FRITTERS A basic fritter recipe is an excellent tool for showcasing all sorts of vegetables. Sweet potatoes, beets, sweet corn, parsnips, and hearty greens are all great options. Here I use a combination of zucchini and carrots. The fritters are very tasty on their own, but the grated lemon zest, goat cheese, and basil sprinkled on top while they're still hot from the pan—oh man! Those simple touches truly elevate this dish.

1½ pounds zucchini (about 3 medium), ends trimmed

1 pound carrots (about 5 medium), peeled and ends trimmed

1 large onion

Kosher salt

3 large eggs, beaten

1 teaspoon finely chopped fresh basil, plus ½ cup thinly sliced fresh basil for garnish

Freshly ground black pepper

1 cup tapioca flour (see Note)

1 teaspoon baking powder

Olive oil

Zest of 2 lemons, for garnish

Mild aged goat cheese, such as Naked Goat, for garnish

1. Using either the grating attachment on a food processor or a handheld box grater, grate the zucchini, carrots, and onion. In a large bowl, toss the grated vegetables with 2 teaspoons salt. Transfer the vegetables to a colander (set the bowl aside) and let them sit for 10 minutes. Wrap the vegetables in a clean dish towel and twist the towel to squeeze out the excess moisture. Return the vegetables to the large bowl.

2. Add the eggs, finely chopped basil, and 1 teaspoon pepper to the vegetables and stir well. Sift in the tapioca flour and baking powder, then stir until blended.

3. Heat a large nonstick skillet over medium heat. Drizzle enough olive oil into the hot skillet to coat the bottom. Working in batches, scoop the batter into the skillet, ¼ cup per fritter, flattening it with the back of the measuring cup. Cook until golden brown on the bottom, 4 to 5 minutes. Flip the fritters over and cook until the second side is golden brown, 2 to 3 minutes. Transfer to a plate and immediately grate the lemon zest and cheese over them. Sprinkle with the sliced basil. Wipe the skillet clean and repeat with the remaining batter and garnishes. Serve warm.

TAPIOCA FLOUR I love using this gluten-free flour because it creates a light, crispy texture not only for these fritters, but pan-fried meats. Dredge cutlets in a 50/50 mix of tapioca flour and cornstarch for the crispiest crusts.

NATURALLY FERMENTED CARROTS

■ MAKES ABOUT 1 POUND Cultures (no pun intended) all over the world have been fermenting foods for many, many years. Not only does this natural process preserve food, but eating fermented foods is a great way to incorporate probiotics—which aid digestion by helping your gut maintain good bacteria—into your diet. I love making sauerkraut, kimchi, fermented salsas, and fermented vegetables like these carrot sticks. There is no reason to fear fermenting foods at home, but you do need to be diligent about sanitization. You must sanitize the mason jar properly and be careful not to touch the inside of the jar with your hands or with any tools that haven't been sanitized.

Delicious on their own, these tangy, crunchy carrots are an amazing accompaniment to a rich grilled cheese sandwich or added to a salad. Feel free to play with the flavor by adding ingredients like garlic, dill, or hot chiles. I also use the same fermentation technique for cabbage to create kimchi and sauerkraut.

Kosher salt

1 pound carrots, peeled

1 (1- to 1½-inch) piece fresh ginger, peeled and sliced into thin coins

½ teaspoon coriander seeds

½ teaspoon whole black peppercorns

1 large cabbage leaf, stem removed, or a sterilized fermentation weight (see Note)

1. Sterilize a quart-size mason jar and a ring lid. You can do this by either boiling them in a pot of water for 10 minutes (be sure that the jars are covered by at least 2 inches of water) or by washing them in the dishwasher on the "sanitizing" setting.

2. Bring 8 cups water to a boil in medium saucepan over high heat. Add 2 tablespoons salt and stir until it has dissolved. Let the water boil rapidly for at least 1 minute and then remove the pan from the heat. Let the brine cool to room temperature.

3. Meanwhile, cut the carrots to fit the mason jar with at least 2 inches of space between the tops of the carrots and the jar lid. (If your carrots are thick or depending on your preference, feel free to cut them in half or quarters lengthwise as well.) Put the carrots into the jar and add the ginger, coriander seeds, and peppercorns.

4. Once the brine has reached room temperature, pour it into the jar to cover the carrots, making sure that the carrots are fully submerged in the brine. (There will be extra brine; just discard it. The proportion of salt to water is important.) Place a fermentation weight on top of the carrots, or if you do not have a fermentation weight, roll the cabbage leaf and shove it into the mason jar to keep the carrots submerged. Place the cheesecloth over the rim of the jar, using the ring lid to secure the cheesecloth. If you are using an airlock lid, simply place that lid over the jar. Put the jar in a cool, dark place to ferment.

5. After a day or so, tiny bubbles should appear in the brine. Begin checking the carrots after 5 days. They will have a tangy, yogurt-like smell due to the lacto-fermentation. Skim off and discard any foam that may have developed. Using a sterilized fork, fish out a carrot stick and taste it. If it is fermented to your liking, discard the cabbage (if you used it) and move the carrots to the fridge. They will continue to ferment, but the process will slow down drastically. The carrots can be fermented at room temperature for up to 10 days. The fermented carrots will keep in the refrigerator for up to 1 month.

FERMENTATION TIPS   Do not skip the step of boiling the water. Not only does boiling kill any potentially harmful bacteria, but it gets rid of trace amounts of chlorine that are added to municipal water. That chlorine can inhibit the *Lactobacilli* bacteria from reproducing and fermenting your vegetables.

The ideal temperature range for fermenting food is 60°F to 70°F. I like to keep my jars in a cupboard while they ferment because it's dark and I'm reminded to check on them. If your house is slightly warmer than 70°F, the fermentation process will likely speed up.

A fermentation weight is a small piece of glass or ceramic that's designed to keep the vegetables submerged in the fermenting medium. They come in different sizes, so make sure to choose one that fits your fermenting vessel.

ROASTED DELICATA SQUASH AND GRAPES

WITH BURRATA

■ SERVES 4 TO 6   Delicata squash is one of my favorite winter squashes, both for its flavor and for the fact that you don't have to peel its thin skin. The combination of roasted squash and roasted grapes is already quite autumnal, and the warming heat of garam masala only heightens that cozy feeling. I always find burrata irresistible, but when it's combined with sweet-savory, hot-from-the-oven squash and grapes, you have a dish that's worth curling up with. This is wonderful as an appetizer or as a side dish.

1 pound delicata squash

2 tablespoons olive oil

1 teaspoon maple syrup

½ teaspoon garam masala

Kosher salt and freshly ground black pepper

8 ounces seedless red grapes, cut into small clusters

1 teaspoon grated lemon zest

8 ounces burrata cheese

Extra-virgin olive oil, for garnish

1. Preheat the oven to 425°F. Line a rimmed baking sheet with parchment paper.

2. Cut the ends off each delicata squash, then cut the squash in half lengthwise. Using a spoon, scrape out the seeds and save them for another use (see Note). Cut the squash into ½-inch-thick half-moons.

3. In a large bowl, whisk together the olive oil, maple syrup, garam masala, ¼ teaspoon salt, and ½ teaspoon pepper. Add the squash and the grapes, and toss to coat. Pour the mixture onto the prepared baking sheet and spread it out into an even layer.

4. Roast, flipping the squash and rotating the baking sheet after 10 minutes (don't bother flipping the grapes), until the squash is soft and golden brown and the grapes are soft and juicy, 20 to 25 minutes. Remove the baking sheet from the oven and sprinkle the lemon zest evenly over the squash and grapes.

5. Divide the burrata among four plates and drizzle a few drops of extra-virgin olive oil over the cheese. Evenly divide the squash and grapes among the four plates. Serve immediately.

ROASTED SQUASH SEEDS   Pumpkin seeds aren't the only squash seeds that you can eat. You can save those delicata seeds and roast them for a snack! Simply rinse the squash flesh off them, pat them dry, and toss them in a neutral oil and your choice of seasoning. You can go the savory route and opt for salt and pepper, or the sweet route with cinnamon and sugar. There are any number of combinations that would be delicious. Let your imagination take flight! Roast the seeds in a preheated 300°F oven until they are lightly browned, 20 to 25 minutes. Store in a sealed container at room temperature for up to 1 week.

Roasted Delicata Squash
and Grapes with Burrata

WILD MUSHROOM FARROTTO

1½ cups farro

2 tablespoons unsalted butter

3 tablespoons extra-virgin olive oil

1 large onion, chopped (about 2 cups)

3 garlic cloves, minced

1 cup dry white wine

1 quart chicken stock, homemade (see page 68) or store-bought, warmed

8 ounces chanterelle mushrooms or other wild mushrooms, stemmed and torn by hand into bite-size pieces

8 ounces cremini mushrooms, stemmed and sliced

Kosher salt

1 tablespoon finely chopped fresh parsley

Freshly ground black pepper

¼ cup grated Parmesan cheese, plus more for serving

2 ounces Fontina cheese, shredded (about ½ cup)

1 tablespoon minced fresh thyme

■ SERVES 8 When I began to learn how to cook, my favorite dish to make was risotto. It was always a crowd-pleaser and it's the perfect example of learning a method rather than a recipe. Sauté the aromatics, toast the rice, add stock, possibly wine, and stir, stir, stir! In half an hour, you end up with a creamy, pasta-like dish that is incredibly comforting. You can change it up based on what's in season and what you have on hand. Once I learned the method of cooking risotto, I could whip it up at any time with confidence. In fact, the first time I appeared on the *Today* show was when I was twenty years old, and I cooked a pork tenderloin and persimmon risotto during a Thanksgiving week episode!

This version of risotto is made with farro instead of the traditional Arborio rice. I like using the farro for a few reasons: It adds a wonderful bite and it delivers more nutrition in the form of a whole grain. It also has a naturally nutty taste that complements the wild mushrooms well. In an issue of *Cook's Illustrated* magazine, I learned the technique of breaking up the farro to produce a creamy texture that mimics the creaminess of traditional risotto. The best part is, unlike a traditional risotto, you don't have to constantly stir it!

1. Place the farro in either a food processor or a blender and pulse about 10 times, until it is broken into smaller pieces.

2. Heat a medium Dutch oven over medium-high heat. Add 1 tablespoon of the butter and 1 tablespoon of the olive oil. When the foaming of the butter subsides, add the onion and half the garlic. Cook, stirring occasionally, until the onion is soft and translucent, 3 to 5 minutes. Add the farro and cook, stirring, until toasted, about 3 minutes. Add the wine and cook, stirring, until most of the liquid has cooked off. Add the warmed chicken stock and reduce the heat to medium-low. Cover the pot and cook, stirring at least once during the cooking time, until the farro is mostly cooked but still chewy, 20 minutes.

3. Meanwhile, heat a large skillet over medium-high heat. Add the remaining 1 tablespoon butter and 1 tablespoon of the olive oil, swirling the pan to coat the bottom. When the foaming of the butter subsides, add all the mushrooms and sear without disturbing them for 1 minute. Cook, stirring occasionally, until the mushrooms release their liquid, 5 minutes. Season them with ½ teaspoon salt and cook until most of the moisture is cooked out of the mushrooms, 3 minutes. Add the remaining 1 tablespoon olive oil and remaining garlic. Cook, stirring, until fragrant, 1 minute, then remove the skillet from the heat. Stir in the chopped parsley and set the mushrooms aside, still in the skillet, until the farrotto is finished.

4. Uncover the farrotto. Stir in 1 teaspoon salt and 1 teaspoon pepper. Cook, uncovered, until the farrotto reaches your desired consistency: about 5 minutes will result in a brothier dish, and 10 minutes will cook off most of the liquid for a thicker farrotto. Taste and season with salt and pepper as desired. Remove the pot from the heat and stir in the cooked mushrooms, Parmesan, Fontina, and thyme. Serve immediately, sprinkled with more Parmesan.

VEGETARIAN   To make a vegetarian version of this dish, substitute a good vegetable stock for the chicken stock. You may want to add more salt and pepper, and possibly more cheese, at the end.

Wild Mushroom Farrotto

SNACKS & BITES

SPINACH ARTICHOKE DIP

■ MAKES 6 CUPS One of my favorite weekend pastimes during the fall and early winter is watching football and spending the day cooking. I have a television right off the kitchen so I can cheer on my Raiders or Cal Bears while I'm preparing long-simmering stews or stocks, grains, and other staples for the upcoming week.

I don't know about you, but I can't enjoy football without some snacks. Most tailgating snacks are loaded with saturated fat, calories, and other junk, but I've come up with a great spinach dip that is packed with protein, veggies, and big flavors. Ground porcini mushrooms are the secret ingredient to boost that umami flavor. Any vegetable crudités would be nice alongside this dip, but chilled Belgian endive and crisp romaine leaves work particularly well to scoop it up.

5 or 6 dried porcini mushrooms

1 tablespoon olive oil

1 large onion, chopped (about 2 cups)

1 (10-ounce) package frozen chopped spinach, thawed

1 (8-ounce) package frozen artichoke hearts, thawed

1 large carrot, peeled and finely grated (about 1 cup)

Kosher salt

⅛ teaspoon cayenne pepper

2 cups 2% or full-fat Greek yogurt

½ cup mayonnaise

1 tablespoon garlic granules

1 tablespoon grated lemon zest (from 1 lemon)

Freshly ground black pepper

1 (5-ounce) can water chestnuts, drained and chopped

1. Using either a spice grinder or a mortar and pestle, grind the porcini mushrooms into a fine powder. Measure out and reserve 2 teaspoons of the mushroom powder.

2. Heat a large skillet over medium heat. Add the olive oil and onion and cook, stirring occasionally, until the onion is soft and translucent, 3 to 5 minutes. Add the spinach, artichoke hearts, carrot, ½ teaspoon salt, and the cayenne. Cook, stirring, until all the liquid has evaporated and the vegetables are heated through, 5 to 8 minutes.

3. Transfer the vegetable mixture to a food processor and pulse it a few times. Scrape down the sides of the bowl and pulse a few more times, until the vegetables are finely chopped and well combined. Let the mixture cool in the processor for at least 10 minutes.

4. Add the 2 teaspoons mushroom powder, the yogurt, mayonnaise, garlic granules, lemon zest, ½ teaspoon black pepper, and ½ teaspoon salt to the cooled vegetables. Pulse a few times, until well combined. Taste and season with more salt and black pepper as desired.

5. Transfer the mixture to a large bowl and fold in the water chestnuts. Refrigerate, covered, for at least 1 hour before serving. The dip will keep in an airtight container in the refrigerator for up to 3 days.

OLIVE FRITTE

■ MAKES 20 OLIVES These olives were served at our wedding rehearsal dinner at Bistro Don Giovanni in Napa Valley. Many of our family members claimed to hate both olives and anchovies, but they ate these with gusto—they're delicious and so addictive. Years later, I met Donna Scala, chef and co-owner of the restaurant, and she let me in on a little secret: olive *fritte* are incredibly easy to make! I like to whip these up as a salty bite to snack on while enjoying an aperitif or sparkling wine with friends.

20 Castelvetrano olives, pitted

4 olive oil–packed anchovy fillets, minced

1 cup buttermilk

½ cup fine dried bread crumbs or cornmeal

Kosher salt and freshly ground black pepper

1 to 2 cups vegetable oil, for frying

¼ cup Marcona almonds

1½ teaspoons finely chopped fresh rosemary leaves

1. Stuff each olive with about ⅛ teaspoon of the minced anchovy.

2. Pour the buttermilk into a shallow bowl. In a separate shallow bowl, combine the bread crumbs, ⅛ teaspoon salt, and ¼ teaspoon pepper. Put all the olives in the bowl of buttermilk and roll them around to cover with the buttermilk. Using a slotted spoon, and being careful to drain them very well, transfer the olives to the bowl of seasoned bread crumbs. Roll them around until they are fully coated (the coating should be thin; if it's too caked on, it may not stick to the olive once it's in the hot oil).

3. Set a wire rack on a baking sheet and place several layers of paper towels on top of the rack.

4. Heat the vegetable oil in a medium pot over medium-high heat. The oil is ready to fry when you insert the handle of a wooden spoon into the oil and the oil bubbles up. Working in batches, shake any excess bread crumbs from the olives and add the olives to the hot oil. The oil will bubble vigorously. Fry the olives, stirring them frequently, until they are golden brown, about 30 seconds. Using a spider strainer or a slotted spoon, transfer the olives to the paper towels. Season them lightly with salt and pepper (keeping in mind that olives are already salty), and let them drain.

5. In a serving bowl, toss the olives with the Marcona almonds and rosemary. Serve immediately.

AVOCADO CILANTRO HUMMUS

1 cup dried chickpeas

1 teaspoon baking soda

2 cups arugula (or baby spinach, or a combination of the two)

¾ cup coarsely chopped fresh cilantro (about ½ bunch)

1 scallion, finely chopped

1 large garlic clove, minced

¼ cup fresh lime juice (from about 2 limes)

1 ripe avocado, pitted, peeled, and coarsely chopped

½ cup olive oil

Kosher salt and freshly ground pepper

■ MAKES 3½ TO 4 CUPS Hummus is such a reliably satisfying, easy, high-protein snack that I often have some around. By making my own, I can vary the flavors to my heart's content. Cooking dried chickpeas takes some time, but it's completely worth it because the taste and texture are far better than that of the canned kind. Plus, the process is mostly hands-off, and you can always cook a large batch of chickpeas ahead of time. Simply drain and cool the cooked chickpeas, place them in a large plastic zip-top bag, and lay the bag flat in the freezer. The frozen cooked chickpeas will keep for about 1 year.

That said, if you are craving some hummus and didn't plan ahead, feel free to substitute rinsed canned chickpeas. You will need 3 cups drained cooked chickpeas for this recipe, which is about a 20-ounce can.

Serve the hummus with crudités or pita chips, or use it as a hearty spread in a sandwich or wrap, such as the Hummus-Avocado Collard Green Wraps on page 102.

1. In a large bowl, combine the chickpeas, baking soda, and 4 cups water. Set the bowl in the refrigerator and let the chickpeas soak for at least 8 hours or up to overnight.

2. Drain and rinse the soaked chickpeas. Place the chickpeas in a large pot and add water to cover by at least 2 inches. Bring it to a boil, then reduce the heat to medium-low. Simmer, partially covered, until the chickpeas are soft, 1½ to 2 hours. Drain and let cool.

3. In a food processor, combine the arugula, cilantro, scallion, garlic, and lime juice. Pulse a few times, scrape down the sides of the bowl, and pulse a few more times, until the mixture is well combined. Add the chickpeas and the avocado. Turn the processor on and slowly add the olive oil in a steady stream. Add 1½ teaspoons salt and 1 teaspoon pepper. Continue to process until the mixture has reached your desired consistency. Taste and season with more salt and pepper as desired. The hummus will keep in an airtight container in the refrigerator for 3 to 5 days, and the flavor will continue to develop over time.

SLOW COOKER CHICKPEAS An easy method of cooking dried chickpeas is to use a slow cooker. Here's the technique, adapted slightly from Alton Brown's method (of course he figured it out!). In the pot of a slow cooker, combine 1 pound dried chickpeas, 1 teaspoon salt, ¼ teaspoon baking soda, and 7 cups water. Cover and cook on High for 4 hours or on Low for 7 to 8 hours. The chickpeas will keep in an airtight container—in their cooking liquid—in the refrigerator for up to 1 week.

MANGO GUACAMOLE

■ MAKES 4 TO 5 CUPS   For my 30th birthday, my husband, friends, and I spent a weekend at a beach house in Santa Cruz, California. Normally I don't make a big deal of my birthday, but 30 was worth celebrating and I was just back from the London Olympics and desperate to spend some quality time with my loved ones in a stress-free environment. It was a perfect weekend filled with friends, beach time, dancing, and, of course, good food.

One afternoon, my husband started blending avocados, mangos, limes, and more, and came up with a guacamole that was a huge hit. I wasn't really paying attention, and neither was he, so this is my best attempt at re-creating that delicious dip. Normally I prefer my guacamole chunky, but this one is best blended in a food processor. Not only does the processor lighten the texture, but when the avocado and mango are combined, the guacamole becomes lightly sweet and creamy. But don't bother adding the mangos unless you have very ripe ones; the hard green ones aren't sweet or flavorful and won't blend well. I love to eat this dip with salty tortilla chips, though it's a really great topping for fish tacos, too.

4 ripe avocados

½ cup fresh lime juice (from about 4 limes)

¼ cup full-fat Greek yogurt

1½ large ripe mangos, peeled, seeded, and chopped (about 2½ cups)

½ red onion, finely chopped

2 serrano chiles, seeded and finely chopped

1½ tablespoons finely chopped fresh cilantro

Kosher salt and freshly ground black pepper

1. Pit and peel the avocados. In a large bowl, using a fork or a potato masher, mash together the avocado flesh and lime juice. Stir in the yogurt, mangos, onion, chiles, and cilantro.

2. Transfer the mixture to a food processor and pulse until you have a chunky puree. Add a hefty pinch of salt and a generous amount of pepper, and pulse to combine. Taste and season with more salt and pepper as desired.

3. The guacamole will keep in an airtight container in the refrigerator for up to 1 day. To prevent it from turning brown, press a piece of plastic wrap directly on the surface of the guacamole, without any air gaps, before closing the container.

RIPE AVOCADOS   Here's a trick for finding a perfectly ripe avocado: Use your index finger to remove the stem nub. If the nub comes out easily and a bright green crater remains, the avocado is perfectly ripe. If the nub doesn't dislodge easily, the avocado is not fully ripe. If the crater is brown, the avocado is overripe.

ROASTED PIQUILLO PEPPER AND GARLIC HUMMUS

■ MAKES 3½ TO 4 CUPS I love the combination of roasted peppers and roasted garlic in this hummus. Roasting garlic is one of the simplest, most delicious tasks, producing a velvety, versatile spread that's full of flavor while perfuming your whole kitchen with its heady aroma. The piquillo peppers aren't spicy but are rich and earthy, a perfect match for the garlic and chickpeas. While great as a dip with crudités, this is also a fantastic spread for a turkey sandwich—or for Hummus-Avocado Collard Green Wraps (page 102). However you enjoy the hummus, it's a very tasty way to load up on fiber and protein.

1 cup dried chickpeas

1 teaspoon baking soda

1 head of garlic

½ cup plus 1 tablespoon extra-virgin olive oil

1 (8-ounce) jar roasted piquillo peppers, drained

¼ cup fresh lemon juice (from about 2 lemons)

Kosher salt and freshly ground black pepper

1. In a large bowl, combine the chickpeas, baking soda, and 4 cups water. Set the bowl in the refrigerator and let the chickpeas soak for at least 8 hours or up to overnight.

2. Drain and rinse the soaked chickpeas. Place the chickpeas in a large pot and add water to cover by at least 2 inches. Bring it to a boil, then reduce the heat to a medium-low. Simmer, partially covered, until they are soft, 1½ to 2 hours. Drain and let cool. (See the Note on page 123 for cooking the chickpeas in a slow cooker.)

3. Meanwhile, preheat the oven to 400°F.

4. Cut off the top ¼ inch of the head of garlic to expose the cloves. Place the garlic on a piece of aluminum foil and drizzle with 1 tablespoon of the olive oil. Wrap the garlic in the foil and place it in the oven. Roast for 30 minutes.

••• recipe continues •••

Avocado Cilantro Hummus

5. Remove the garlic from the oven and carefully open the foil to check it; the garlic is ready when the cloves are lightly caramelized and very soft. If it isn't ready, rewrap it and continue to roast it in 5-minute intervals, checking after each. When the garlic is fully roasted, remove it from the oven, open the foil, and let it cool slightly. When it is cool enough to handle, squeeze the roasted cloves out of the skins directly into a food processor. Discard the skins.

6. To the food processor, add the cooked chickpeas, piquillo peppers, and lemon juice. Pulse several times until well combined, scraping down the sides of the bowl as necessary. With the machine running, drizzle in the remaining ½ cup olive oil. Add the 1½ teaspoons salt and 1 teaspoon black pepper, and pulse a few more times. Taste and season with more salt and black pepper as desired. The hummus will keep in an airtight container in the refrigerator for 3 to 5 days.

Roasted Piquillo Pepper
and Garlic Hummus

GRANDMA'S LUMPIA

■ MAKES ABOUT 40 LUMPIA Lumpia—essentially a Filipino version of a fried spring roll—are synonymous with my family's celebrations. My grandma makes a huge batch of them for every Thanksgiving and Christmas, as well as for most of our other get-togethers. My cousins and I adore them—so much so that Grandma will ration them throughout the hors d'oeuvres hour so we don't spoil our dinner. She knows we would!

There are countless versions of lumpia, and while I've tried and liked quite a few, my grandma's are the best (naturally!). Resist the urge to overfill them; if they are too full, they won't cook evenly inside and out. Lumpia are much smaller than Chinese egg rolls and should not be any larger than 4 inches long and just shy of 1 inch in diameter (no bigger than a cigar). Since assembly is somewhat labor-intensive, we often make two or three batches at a time, freezing the extra for later. To freeze them, put the assembled (but not yet fried) lumpia on a baking sheet with space between them and freeze them overnight. The next day, transfer them to a plastic zip-top bag and store in the freezer for up to 6 months. To cook, there's no need to defrost them first; just add 1 to 2 minutes to the frying time.

1 pound lean ground pork

1½ cups finely chopped onions

1 (8-ounce) can water chestnuts, drained and finely chopped

2 tablespoons minced garlic

2 tablespoons liquid Maggi seasoning (see Note) or soy sauce

1 tablespoon ground white pepper

2 tablespoons cornstarch

30 to 45 lumpia wrappers (see Note)

Vegetable oil, for deep-frying

Thai sweet chili sauce, for serving

1. In a large bowl, combine the pork, onions, water chestnuts, garlic, Maggi seasoning, and white pepper. Using your hands, mix thoroughly.

2. In a small bowl, whisk together the cornstarch and ⅓ cup water.

3. Gently separate the lumpia wrappers (they're very delicate), arrange them on a clean work surface, and cover them with a clean damp dish towel or paper towels to prevent them from drying out. Keep the wrappers covered while you are assembling each lumpia. To assemble one, place a wrapper on a cutting board. Using a pastry brush or your finger, moisten the top edge of the wrapper (the one farthest from you) with the cornstarch mixture. Place 2 tablespoons of the pork mixture along the center of the wrapper, forming a log shape. Bring the bottom edge of the wrapper up over the log, pulling it tightly, and then fold the left and right sides of the wrapper toward the center over the log. Tightly roll up the lumpia and press to seal

the edge. Place the lumpia on a plate, cover it with plastic wrap, and repeat with the remaining wrappers and filling.

4. Set a wire rack on a baking sheet and place several layers of paper towels on top of the rack.

5. Heat 3 to 4 inches of vegetable oil in a large wok or pot to 375°F. (If you don't have a thermometer, test the oil by inserting the handle of a wooden spoon into the oil. If bubbles appear immediately, the oil is ready.) Working in batches, deep-fry the lumpia, using tongs to flip them over halfway through, until they are a deep golden brown all over, about 3 minutes total. Using a spider strainer or a slotted spoon, transfer the lumpia to the paper towels to drain.

6. Serve the lumpia warm with the sweet chili sauce for dipping.

MAGGI   Maggi seasoning is what my grandma uses to season her lumpia, and it is readily available in the international section of most grocery stores. If you cannot find it, feel free to substitute soy sauce.

WRAPPERS   If you can't find lumpia wrappers, Chinese spring roll wrappers will work, too. They are similar, but they tend to be less delicate than the traditional Filipino lumpia wrappers. For Fresh Lumpia (page 132), the Chinese spring roll ones are actually preferable, because they make rolling the lumpia much easier! (Make sure to get the Chinese variety, which are wheat flour–based, versus other spring roll wrappers or skins that are rice flour–based.)

OVEN-FRIED LUMPIA   You can also "oven-fry" the lumpia: Spray a rimmed baking sheet with cooking spray and arrange the lumpia on the baking sheet with an inch of space between them. Spray the lumpia with cooking spray. Bake in a preheated 425°F oven until deep golden brown, 20 to 25 minutes.

Grandma's Lumpia

FRESH LUMPIA

■ MAKES ABOUT 25 LUMPIA The fried (or oven-fried) version of lumpia (see page 128) will always be my favorite, but there are times when you want something a little lighter. Here is a version of the Filipino snack that's similar to a fresh spring roll. These lumpia are much larger and more delicate than the fried ones. The butter lettuce not only adds a freshness and crunch but also protects the delicate wrapper from the cooked filling during assembly. The sweet, savory sauce drizzled on at the end softens and "cooks" the wrapper. I love garlic, but if you're not a fan, feel free to omit it in the sauce.

LUMPIA FILLING

1 (16-ounce) package extra-firm tofu, drained and cut into ½-inch cubes

1 tablespoon annatto seeds (see Note)

4 tablespoons vegetable oil

⅓ pound boneless pork loin, cut into ½-inch cubes

1 large onion, chopped (about 2 cups)

3 garlic cloves, minced

8 ounces green beans, trimmed and cut into ½-inch pieces

1 pound Yukon Gold potatoes, peeled and cut into ¼-inch cubes

8 ounces shrimp, peeled and deveined, cut into ½-inch cubes

2 cups shredded napa cabbage

¼ cup full-fat unsweetened coconut milk

1 tablespoon chicken stock base (I like Better Than Bouillon)

Freshly ground black pepper

Soy sauce or tamari, for seasoning

1. **Prepare the lumpia filling** Spread the tofu cubes out on several layers of paper towels and let sit for 30 minutes to drain off as much liquid as possible.

2. Meanwhile, rinse the annatto seeds in a fine-mesh sieve, drain, and put them in a bowl. Add ¼ cup water and let the seeds soak for at least 30 minutes.

3. Strain the annatto soaking liquid through a fine-mesh sieve into a bowl, pressing on the seeds with the back of a spoon to extract as much color as possible. Reserve the colored soaking liquid and discard the seeds.

4. In a large wok or saucepan, heat 2 tablespoons of the vegetable oil over medium-high heat. Add the drained tofu and cook, stirring occasionally, until the cubes are golden brown and crisp, 5 to 7 minutes. Don't worry if some of the tofu sticks to the bottom of the pan. Transfer the tofu to a plate.

5. To the same pan, add the remaining 2 tablespoons vegetable oil and the pork. Cook, stirring occasionally, until the meat is almost cooked through, about 5 minutes. Add the onion and cook, stirring, until it is softened and translucent, about 5 minutes. Add the garlic and cook, stirring constantly, for 1 minute. Add the green beans and potatoes and cook, stirring, until they are almost cooked through, 4 to 6 minutes. Add the annatto soaking liquid, the shrimp, cabbage, coconut milk, and chicken stock base.

2 cups chicken stock, homemade (see page 68) or store-bought

1 tablespoon soy sauce or tamari

3 garlic cloves, crushed with the side of a knife (optional)

¼ cup sugar

Freshly ground black pepper

2 tablespoons cornstarch dissolved in ¼ cup water

ASSEMBLY

25 to 30 lumpia wrappers (see Note, page 129)

1 head butter lettuce, pulled into leaves, hard center ribs removed

Cook, stirring occasionally, until the shrimp are cooked through and the liquid has cooked off, about 5 minutes. Stir in the cooked tofu. Season with pepper and soy sauce to taste. Remove the pan from the heat and let the filling cool slightly while you make the sauce. If there is any liquid remaining, drain the filling in a strainer (any extra liquid will make assembly quite difficult).

6. **Make the sauce**   In a medium saucepan, combine the chicken stock, soy sauce, garlic (if using), sugar, and ¼ teaspoon pepper. Bring to a boil, whisking to make sure the sugar dissolves. Boil until the sauce has reduced by half, 5 minutes. Add the cornstarch slurry and cook until the mixture has thickened, 1 minute. Keep the sauce warm while you assemble the lumpia.

7. **Assemble the lumpia**   The lumpia wrappers are delicate, so pull them apart gently and arrange them on a clean work surface. Keep them covered with a clean damp dish towel or paper towel while you assemble them one by one. Place a lumpia wrapper in front of you so it forms a diamond shape. Place one butter lettuce leaf just off center, toward the left side of the wrapper. (You are going to leave the left edge of the lumpia untucked, so place the leaf so it is overlapping that edge.) Place ¼ cup of the lumpia filling on top of the lettuce leaf. Tuck the right side of the wrapper over the filling and then gently bring the bottom corner over the filling and roll the filling toward the top to close. (Unlike fried lumpia, the fresh version is not tightly wrapped. The filling will tear the wrapper if you wrap too tightly.) Place the lumpia on a platter, seam-side down, and cover it with a damp paper towel. Repeat with the remaining wrappers, lettuce, and filling.

8. To serve, spoon the warm sauce all over the lumpia and enjoy right away.

ANNATTO   If you can't find annatto seeds, just omit them and use ¼ cup water in place of the annatto soaking liquid in step 5. The addition of annatto seeds is more for color than for flavor.

SPICY "CHEESY" POPCORN

■ **SERVES 4** You'd be surprised to know how many movies Olympians watch during peak training. Rest and recovery are paramount to athletic performance, which means many of us have to fill that downtime with entertainment. I don't know about you, but I cannot watch a movie without something to munch on! Here I give popcorn—a whole grain—a healthy twist. Nutritional yeast adds protein, vitamin B$_{12}$, and a great cheesy flavor. When combined with the *shichimi togarashi*—a Japanese spice blend that can be found in quality grocery stores and in Asian markets—it tastes just like Spicy Nacho Doritos, though much better for you.

¼ cup nutritional yeast (see Note)

1 teaspoon *shichimi togarashi* (Japanese spice blend), plus more as desired

1 teaspoon garlic granules

Kosher salt

1 tablespoon grapeseed oil or other high-heat neutral oil (see page 20)

½ cup popcorn kernels

2 tablespoons extra-virgin olive oil

1. In a spice grinder, combine the nutritional yeast, *shichimi togarashi*, garlic granules, and 1 teaspoon salt. Process until you have a fine powder.

2. Set a large pot over medium-high heat. Add the grapeseed oil and 3 kernels of popcorn to the pot and cover the pot. When the 3 kernels have popped, add the remaining kernels and cover the pot again. Shake it vigorously every few seconds while you wait for the popping to start and then during the popping. When the popping has slowed down to a few seconds between pops (this will take about 4 minutes), remove the pot from the heat and pour the popped popcorn into a large bowl.

3. Pour the olive oil over the popcorn and toss well. Add the spiced yeast mixture and toss to combine. Taste and season with more *shichimi togarashi* and salt as desired. Serve immediately.

NUTRITIONAL YEAST This flaky, savory seasoning can be purchased at quality grocery stores and health food stores. I love it because it adds a cheesy flavor without any dairy, making it a great option for vegans or people who can't handle lactose. It adds vitamin B$_{12}$ to your diet, something that vegetarians and vegans often lack. Plus, it's shelf stable, so I always have some on hand.

PEANUT BUTTER ENERGY BITES

■ MAKES ABOUT 20 BITES During high school, I made myself a peanut butter and jelly sandwich to eat for lunch nearly every day. The lack of diversity in my midday meal drove my mom crazy, but nothing she tried managed to break my PB&J habit (until senior year, when she started making my lunch for me!). My culinary skills have drastically improved since those days, but I still love peanut butter.

These snack bites are a great option for healthy between-meal nibbling, as they're packed with protein, fiber, healthy fats, and minerals. They are portable and can be enjoyed before, during, or after a workout to help sustain your energy level.

½ cup natural whole (raw) almonds

1½ cups old-fashioned rolled oats

4 pitted Medjool dates

½ cup smooth natural peanut butter

1 tablespoon honey

1 tablespoon ground flaxseed

1 tablespoon ground cinnamon

½ teaspoon pink Himalayan salt

½ cup popped amaranth (see Note) or other popped cereal

1. In a food processor, process the almonds until they resemble coarse sand, about 30 seconds. Add 1 cup of the oats and pulse until the almonds and oats are pulverized, 8 to 10 pulses. Add the remaining ½ cup oats and pulse a few more times. (Adding the rolled oats in stages gives the bites a nice variation in texture). Add the dates, peanut butter, honey, flaxseed, cinnamon, and salt. Pulse until the mixture is well combined. Add ½ cup water and process until the mixture forms a sticky dough.

2. Place the popped amaranth in a medium bowl. Scoop up the dough by the tablespoon and, using your hands, roll it into balls. Roll the balls around in the amaranth until they are coated. The snack balls will keep in an airtight container in the fridge for up to 1 week.

AMARANTH If you can't find popped amaranth, you can easily make your own. For 1 cup popped amaranth, start with ¼ cup uncooked amaranth. Heat a large skillet over medium-high heat (make sure the skillet is heated fully). Add 2 tablespoons of amaranth to the skillet and cover the pan. The amaranth should start popping after a few seconds. Shake the skillet until nearly all the amaranth is popped, and immediately pour the popped amaranth onto a baking sheet. The amaranth burns quickly, so keep a close eye on it. Repeat until you have enough popped amaranth.

SEAFOOD

SPICY COCONUT MUSSELS

2 tablespoons fresh lime juice (from about 1 lime)

1 teaspoon fish sauce

2 teaspoons palm sugar or granulated sugar

1 tablespoon coconut oil

1 cup thinly sliced shallots (2 to 3 large shallots)

3 garlic cloves, thinly sliced

4 makrut lime leaves (see Note, page 158), stemmed and finely shredded

1 fresh Thai chile, seeded and thinly sliced (or leave the seeds if you like the extra heat)

1 teaspoon *sambal oelek* (see Note, page 158)

½ cup dry white wine

1 (13.5-ounce) can full-fat unsweetened coconut milk

3 pounds mussels, debearded and scrubbed

½ cup chopped fresh cilantro

■ SERVES 2 TO 4   Mussels seem to be one of those seafoods that people order at restaurants but never cook at home. But mussels are excellent for weeknight cooking: they are affordable and cook up in less than 30 minutes. Plus, they're low in fat and a great source of protein and iron.

In this recipe, I make a rich sauce with the brine of the mussels and a spicy coconut milk mixture. I use palm sugar to add a touch of sweetness and because it's a traditional sweetener in Southeast Asian fare, but granulated sugar can be substituted. Serve these with something that will sop up all those wonderful juices; crusty bread, steamed rice, and rice vermicelli noodles are all great options.

1. In a small bowl, whisk together the lime juice, fish sauce, and palm sugar until the sugar has fully dissolved.

2. In a saucepan that's large enough to hold all the mussels, heat the coconut oil over medium heat. When the oil is shimmering, add the shallots and cook, stirring, until they are translucent and softened, about 5 minutes. Reduce the heat to medium-low and add the garlic. Cook, stirring, until it is soft and fragrant, 3 more minutes. Add the lime leaves, chile, and *sambal oelek* and cook, stirring, for 1 more minute. Add the wine and cook, stirring, until the wine has reduced by half, 3 to 5 minutes. Add the coconut milk and cook, stirring occasionally, until the sauce thickens slightly, about 5 minutes.

3. Place a large bowl near the stove to collect the mussels as they cook. Add all the mussels to the pan, stirring to coat them with the sauce. Cover and let cook. After 2 minutes, check to see if any mussels have opened. Remove the mussels as they open and put them in the bowl. If your mussels aren't in one layer in the pan, give them a stir. Continue covering the pan and checking every 30 seconds. Some mussels are more stubborn than others, but discard

any mussels that haven't opened after 8 to 10 minutes.
Divide the mussels among individual serving bowls.

4. Remove the pan from the heat and add the cilantro and the
   lime juice mixture to the cooking liquid. Stir well, then ladle
   the sauce over the mussels. Serve immediately.

HOW TO PREPARE MUSSELS

Make sure to buy mussels from a reputable source and keep them on ice until you get
home (if you ask, the fishmonger will give you a small bag of ice). They're usually sold
alive, so take good care of them. When you get home, take them out of their plastic
bag and place them in a large bowl. Cover them with wet paper towels or a damp
dishcloth and refrigerate them until you're ready to cook them.

When you are ready to cook them, give the mussels a good rinse and scrub, if
needed. If you see any beards, use your fingers to remove them. Discard any mussels
that are chipped or that won't close. If you find a couple that are open, tap them
together and see if they close. If they don't, discard them. Discard any mussels that
smell fishy.

Spicy Coconut Mussels

LONGANISA STEAMER CLAMS

■ SERVES 4 Steamer clams are one of my all-time favorite comfort foods. And they happen to be good for you, too, as they're packed with protein and minerals, including iron. I think it's impossible to improve on the nearly perfect combination of linguine and clams, but I love how versatile clams are. You can change the aromatics and the cooking liquid to come up with any number of flavor variations. This combination reminds me of my great-grandpa because San Miguel was his favorite beer. I like the spice of the red pepper flakes to complement the sweetness of the sausage, but if you don't like the heat, feel free to leave them out. Serve this dish with steamed rice, toasted bread, or pasta to sop up those delicious juices.

1 tablespoon extra-virgin olive oil

6 ounces sweet longanisa sausage (see Note), cut into ¼-inch cubes

½ large onion, chopped (about 1 cup)

1 to 2 teaspoons crushed red pepper flakes (optional)

4 pounds steamer clams

1 cup San Miguel beer or other lager

¼ cup finely chopped fresh parsley

Calamansi wedges (see Note, page 188) or lemon wedges, for garnish

1. Heat a large, wide-bottomed saucepot over medium-high heat. Add the olive oil and longanisa and cook, stirring, until the sausage is browned and crisped, about 5 minutes. Add the onion and red pepper flakes (if using) and cook until the onion is soft and translucent, about 3 minutes.

2. Gently add the clams (the shells crack easily, so be careful), then the beer. Cover and cook for 5 minutes, shaking the pan occasionally. Check the clams and transfer any that have opened to a bowl. Cover the pan and cook, checking the clams occasionally, until all the clams have opened. If any clams haven't opened after 10 to 12 minutes total, discard them. Return all the clams to the pot and add the parsley. Serve with calamansi wedges.

LONGANISA If you can't find this sweet Filipino sausage, feel free to substitute linguiça or Spanish chorizo.

Cooking clams at home is not difficult, I promise! You just need to treat them well and encourage them to purge any sand.

- When you purchase fresh clams, take them out of their plastic bag as soon as you get home; they are alive and need to breathe. Place them in a colander, cover them with a damp dish towel, and refrigerate them.

- About an hour before you're going to cook them, take them out of the fridge and give them a good scrub with your hands or with a scrubbing brush to remove any dirt or debris.

- Put the clams in a large bowl and cover them with a few inches of water. Let them soak for at least 20 minutes, or up to 1 hour, so that they can purge any sand.

- When you are ready to cook them, lift the clams out of the water—don't pour them out along with the water, which would just pour the sand back on them and potentially crack the shells.

LEMONY SOY CRAB NOODLES

■ SERVES 4   In the Bay Area, Dungeness crab season often coincides with the holidays and ends in early spring. Since my husband and I have been together, our Christmas dinner tradition is to have a crab feast. Often we will share two or three crabs with a number of dipping sauces, a fresh baguette, and Champagne. It's not the most balanced meal, but it is *so* good!

My favorite sauce is the simplest one: a 50/50 combo of lemon juice and soy sauce. As an homage to my favorite dipping sauce, and in an effort to create a more balanced main dish that feeds more than two people, I developed this noodle dish. Beware that you make more crab stock than you need for the recipe. Freeze and save the leftover stock for the next time a craving for crab noodles strikes (see Note). If you don't want to make the crab stock yourself, you can substitute a light chicken stock or dashi stock.

CRAB STOCK

2 Dungeness crabs, cooked, cracked, and cleaned, or about 12 ounces jumbo lump crabmeat

1 large onion, halved

2 celery stalks, coarsely chopped

6 garlic cloves

6 dried chiles de árbol or other dried chiles

6 to 8 sprigs fresh thyme

2 bay leaves

1 teaspoon whole black peppercorns

Kosher salt

1. **Make the crab stock**   Separate the meat from the shells of the crabs and pick through it for any cartilage; put the meat in the refrigerator, covered. Put the shells in a large stockpot and add 12 cups water, the onion, celery, garlic, dried chiles, thyme, bay leaves, and peppercorns. Set the pot over high heat, bring to a boil, then reduce the heat to medium-low. Simmer for 90 minutes.

2. Remove the pot from the heat and strain the crab stock. Discard all the solids. Taste the stock and season it with salt as desired. Reserve 1 cup for this recipe, and store the remaining stock in the freezer for the next time you make these noodles (let the stock cool first, then pack it in freezer-safe containers and store it in the freezer for up to 6 months).

3. **Prepare the stir-fry sauce**   In a small bowl, whisk 1 tablespoon of the crab stock with the cornstarch until smooth.

4. Using a vegetable peeler, remove the lemon zest in strips, being careful to avoid the bitter white pith. (Reserve the

1 teaspoon cornstarch

1 lemon

2 tablespoons soy sauce or tamari, plus more as desired

1 teaspoon sugar

Chinese egg noodles, fresh or dried (see Note)

1 tablespoon toasted sesame oil

1 tablespoon grapeseed oil or other high-heat neutral oil (see page 20)

1 teaspoon grated fresh ginger

4 scallions, finely chopped

1 fresh Thai chile, finely chopped

½ cup sliced water chestnuts

peeled lemon for serving.) In a small saucepan, combine the lemon zest, remaining reserved crab stock, soy sauce, and sugar. Bring to a boil over medium-high heat, then reduce the heat to medium-low. Simmer to allow the flavors to infuse the stock, 20 minutes. Add the cornstarch mixture and simmer until the sauce has thickened slightly, 2 minutes. Taste and season with more soy sauce as desired. Remove from the heat.

5. Cook the egg noodles to al dente according to the package directions. Drain the noodles and toss them with the sesame oil. Using clean kitchen shears, cut the noodles a few times to shorten them so that they won't get too tangled during stir-frying.

6. Heat a cast-iron pan or a wok over medium-high heat. Add the grapeseed oil, ginger, half the scallions, and the fresh chile. Cook, stirring often to avoid burning, for 1 minute. Add the noodles and stir-fry until they are coated in and have absorbed some of the oil, 1 to 2 minutes. A little browning of the noodles is okay, but avoid burning the aromatics. Add the reserved crabmeat, the stir-fry sauce, remaining scallions, and water chestnuts. Toss and stir-fry until the crab is heated through, 1 to 2 minutes.

7. Divide the noodles among four bowls, squeeze a little of the reserved lemon over them, and serve immediately.

CRAB STOCK   To simplify this noodle dish, make the crab stock in advance and freeze it. It will keep for 6 months. If you make a dish with fresh crab, save the shells in a plastic zip-top bag in the freezer until you're ready to make the stock.

NOODLES   Fresh Chinese egg noodles are much better than the version that we see in little dried bricks. In better grocery stores, you can find them in the refrigerated section. Otherwise, I like to make a trip to an Asian market, stock up on good-quality noodles, and store them in my freezer. No need to defrost before cooking; just cook them for 30 to 60 seconds longer than you normally would.

SHRIMP FRITTERS

DIPPING SAUCE

3 tablespoons Filipino cane vinegar or rice vinegar

2 tablespoons soy sauce or tamari

1 garlic clove, minced into a paste

⅛ teaspoon sugar

FRITTERS

1¼ cups cornstarch

¼ cup all-purpose flour, plus more if needed

1 (1-ounce) packet Lipton onion soup mix

¼ teaspoon baking powder

1 large egg, beaten

Freshly ground black pepper

8 ounces shrimp (25/30 count), peeled and deveined, cut into 1-inch chunks

1½ cups mung bean sprouts

1 cup grated peeled carrot (about 1 large carrot)

1 cup grated peeled sweet potato (about ½ small sweet potato)

Canola oil, for frying

Kosher salt

■ MAKES 20 TO 25 FRITTERS   I was very fortunate to have both of my grandma's parents in my life until I was in college. When my great-grandma passed, she and my great-grandpa had been married for sixty-nine years. He passed soon after her. At the time, they had twenty-six grandchildren and ten great-grandchildren, with more on the way. I was the oldest great-grandchild.

This is my variation of my great-grandma Aguillon's *ukoy* recipe, essentially a Filipino shrimp fritter, which was one of her specialties. The Lipton onion soup mix was my great-grandma's secret ingredient because it adds so much flavor. The sweet-sour vinegar dipping sauce is really delicious with the combination of potato, carrot, and shrimp in the fritter. Filipino cane vinegar is more traditional, but rice vinegar can easily be substituted if you can't find it.

1. **Prepare the dipping sauce**   In a small bowl, whisk together the vinegar, soy sauce, garlic, and sugar until the sugar has dissolved.

2. **Make the fritters**   Place a wire rack over a baking sheet and cover it with several layers of paper towels.

3. In a medium bowl, combine the cornstarch, flour, onion soup mix, and baking powder.

4. In a separate medium bowl, combine ⅔ cup water with the egg and ½ teaspoon pepper and whisk until well blended. Fold in the shrimp, bean sprouts, carrot, and sweet potato. Fold in the cornstarch mixture until it is well incorporated. The mixture should be wetter than a pancake batter but not as thin as a crepe batter. If it is too thin, add a tablespoon or so more all-purpose flour. If it is too thick, add a tablespoon or so of water. At this point, you can cover and refrigerate the batter until you're ready to fry the fritters, but for no longer than 2 hours (more than that and the shrimp and vegetables will start to release water into the batter, which you don't want).

5. Pour about 2 inches of canola oil into a large saucepan or wok, set it over high heat, and heat the oil to about 350°F. To test if the oil is ready to fry, insert the handle of a wooden spoon into the oil; if the oil bubbles up, you're ready to go.

6. Working in batches, using a ¼-cup measuring cup, scoop the batter into the hot oil. (I like to hold the measuring cup in my left hand and use my right hand to slide the batter out with a large spoon.) You want the fritter mixture to bubble vigorously, but not violently, when it hits the oil. If the oil is too hot, the fritter will burn before the inside is cooked; if it is too cool, the fritter will be greasy. Fry until the fritters are golden brown and crisp, 3 to 4 minutes per side. Using a spider or a slotted spoon, transfer the fritters to the prepared baking sheet. Immediately season them with a small pinch of salt. Repeat with the remaining batter, removing any bits and pieces of batter that remain in the oil after each batch.

7. Serve hot, with the dipping sauce on the side.

Shrimp Fritters

SHEET PAN TILAPIA

WITH CHERRY SALSA

■ SERVES 2   There is no easier method for cooking fish fillets than on a baking sheet under the broiler, and I often turn to this technique when I'm exhausted and don't feel like cooking. Preheating the baking sheet ensures that the fish won't stick and gives the fillets a light crust on the bottom. Since you can dress up the cooked fish with any number of simple sauces— an aioli (see page 97), vinaigrette, herb oil, or salsa, just to name a few—it never gets old. I love this cherry salsa because it's sweet yet savory, with a slight kick and a beautiful color. Though if you're just too tired to make a condiment, you can never go wrong with a squeeze of lemon and a drizzle of high-quality extra-virgin olive oil.

CHERRY SALSA

16 Bing cherries, pitted (about ¾ cup; fresh is preferred but frozen works)

½ fresh Thai chile, seeded and coarsely chopped

2 tablespoons sliced scallion, white and light green parts only (about 1 scallion)

2 tablespoons coarsely chopped fresh cilantro

1 tablespoon extra-virgin olive oil

¼ teaspoon balsamic vinegar

Kosher salt and freshly ground black pepper

TILAPIA

2 (6-ounce) tilapia fillets or other mild-flavored thin white-fleshed fish fillets

Kosher salt and freshly ground black pepper

2 tablespoons olive oil

2 lemon wedges, for serving

1. **Prepare the cherry salsa**   In a small food processor, combine the cherries, chile, scallion, cilantro, olive oil, vinegar, ⅛ teaspoon salt, and ⅛ teaspoon pepper. Pulse several times, scrape down the sides of the bowl, and pulse again. Run the food processor until the salsa is blended but still chunky, or to your desired consistency. Taste and season with more salt and pepper as desired.

2. **Cook the tilapia**   Arrange an oven rack about 6 inches from the heating element and preheat the broiler to high. Once the oven is properly heated, place a baking sheet in the oven and let it preheat for at least 5 minutes.

3. Meanwhile, pat the tilapia dry with a paper towel and season each side of the fish with a pinch of salt and a few grinds of pepper.

4. Working quickly, carefully remove the baking sheet from the oven. Drizzle the baking sheet with the olive oil and

place the fillets on the sheet—they should sizzle. Return the baking sheet to the oven and center the fillets under the heating element. Broil for 90 seconds to 3 minutes, keeping an eye on the fish so that it does not overcook. The fish is done when it easily flakes when poked lightly with a fork. Remove the baking sheet from the oven and transfer the fish to serving plates.

5. Squeeze a lemon wedge over each fillet and spoon the salsa over the top. Serve immediately.

VARIATION
LEMON HERB OIL

■ MAKES A SCANT ¼ CUP Fresh-tasting and easy to whip up, this is another of my favorite sauces for this tilapia and can be used in lieu of the cherry salsa.

¼ cup loosely packed fresh basil leaves

1 tablespoon coarsely chopped fresh mint leaves

1 tablespoon grated lemon zest (from about 1 lemon)

2 tablespoons extra-virgin olive oil

Kosher salt and freshly ground black pepper

Using a mortar and pestle, pound the basil and mint until you have a coarse paste. Add the lemon zest and, using a circular motion, grind the herbs and zest together. Add the olive oil, ⅛ teaspoon salt, and ⅛ teaspoon pepper and continue grinding with a circular motion until you have a creamy oil. Taste and season with more salt and pepper as desired. (Alternatively, combine the ingredients in a small food processor and process, scraping the sides of the bowl a couple of times, until creamy.)

Sheet Pan Tilapia with
Cherry Salsa

THAI-STYLE BUTTERFISH EN PAPILLOTE

1 lemongrass stalk

1 teaspoon finely grated fresh ginger

1 scallion, white part only, coarsely chopped

1 tablespoon minced fresh cilantro

2 teaspoons maple syrup

1 teaspoon *sambal oelek* or other chile paste (see Note, page 158)

1 teaspoon soy sauce or tamari

½ teaspoon fish sauce

2 (6-ounce) black cod (butterfish) fillets

Kosher salt

2 makrut lime leaves (see Note, page 158; optional)

3 cups coarsely chopped baby bok choy

Steamed brown rice, for serving

1 lime, cut into wedges, for garnish

■ SERVES 2 *En papillote* means "in a paper packet," and it is one of the easiest, most flavorful ways to cook fish. I like to use aluminum foil because it's a little easier to work with, but feel free to be a purist and use parchment paper. This recipe is one of my favorites, but the possibilities are endless for cooking *en papillote*! You can try citrus slices and shaved fennel, or roasted bell peppers and oil-cured olives, and any number of pestos can be incorporated. You can add any vegetable that can be steamed, such as asparagus, broccoli, fresh peas, and more. This technique should be one of your go-tos for a quick, healthy way to enjoy fish.

Butterfish, also called black cod, is a sustainable option when it comes to seafood, considered by the Monterey Bay Aquarium Seafood Watch as a "best choice." This fish is very high in omega-3 fatty acids, which give it its silky, delicate texture and unmistakable flavor. If you can't find butterfish, substitute any delicate white fish.

1. Place a rack in the center of the oven and preheat the oven to 400°F.

2. Using a sharp knife, cut off the bottom and next 4 to 5 inches of the lemongrass; discard the top and bottom pieces of the stalk. Cut the 4- to 5-inch piece in half lengthwise and discard the woody outer layers. Coarsely chop the softer, pale interior of the lemongrass stalk.

3. Put the lemongrass in a mortar and pestle and add the ginger, scallion, and cilantro. Pound the mixture until you have a coarse paste. (Alternatively, use a small food processor.) Combine the paste with the maple syrup, *sambal oelek*, soy sauce, and fish sauce. Season the fish fillets with salt, then spread half the paste on one fillet and half on the other.

•••• recipe continues ••••

4. Cut two pieces of parchment paper or aluminum foil each about 12 inches long, or large enough to hold half the bok choy and one fish fillet. Place one of the pieces of paper in front of you so it forms a diamond shape. Place the makrut lime leaf (if using) just above the center of the paper. Pile half the bok choy on top of the leaf, followed by a fish fillet. Fold the bottom corner up to meet the top corner and tightly crimp the edges of the packet to seal. Repeat with the remaining lime leaf, bok choy, and fish fillet. Place the packets on a baking sheet.

5. Roast until the fish is cooked through, 20 to 23 minutes, depending on the thickness of the fillets.

6. Divide the rice between two shallow bowls. While holding one of the paper packets above a bowl, carefully tear the paper, being careful of the steam, allowing the juices to spill onto the rice. Gently slide the fish and bok choy onto the rice. Repeat with the second packet. Discard the lime leaves and serve with the lime wedges.

SAMBAL OELEK   This Southeast Asian condiment has lots of fresh chile flavor with slight vinegary undertones. Unlike a lot of other Asian chile pastes, this doesn't have a sweetness. When I don't have a fresh chile on hand for a recipe, I reach for *sambal oelek* as a substitute.

LIME LEAVES   Makrut lime leaves are also known as kaffir lime leaves. They can be found fresh or frozen in better grocery stores and in Asian markets.

POLYNESIAN COCONUT POKE

(POISSON CRU)

■ **SERVES 4** A few years ago I went with several other Olympians to French Polynesia for the Tahiti Swimming Experience and the Polynesian hospitality was incredible. The local people would greet us with music, dancing, flower garlands, and plenty of food. One staple that always appeared on the menu was *poisson cru,* a Polynesian-style *poke.*

On one of our beach excursions, our hosts graciously showed me how to make this dish. They would cut up freshly caught fish, place it in a colander, and take it to the ocean to rinse the fish in the fresh seawater. At home, I rinse the fish in salted water and pretend that I'm basking in the Polynesian sun. Traditionally this is served as a salad, but I like to eat it as an appetizer, serving it like a Peruvian-style ceviche, with plantain chips, taro chips, or potato chips alongside to scoop up the *poke.*

2 tablespoons plus 1 teaspoon pink Himalayan salt

1 pound sashimi-grade ahi tuna, skin and bloodline removed

1 cup full-fat unsweetened coconut milk

1 garlic clove

⅓ cup fresh lemon juice (from about 3 lemons)

1 cup quartered cherry tomatoes

1 large carrot, peeled and grated (about 1 cup)

1 large sweet onion, thinly sliced (about 1 cup)

⅔ cup grated peeled Japanese or Persian cucumber

Freshly ground black pepper

Sliced scallions and sesame seeds, for garnish (optional)

1. In a large bowl, dissolve 2 tablespoons of the salt in 4 cups cool water.

2. Cut the ahi into bite-size pieces (about ¾-inch cubes). Add the ahi to the salted water and give it a good stir. Let the ahi soak for 5 to 10 minutes.

3. In a small bowl, combine the coconut milk and remaining 1 teaspoon salt. Using a Microplane, finely grate the garlic into the coconut milk. Stir well.

4. Drain the ahi, return it to the empty bowl, and stir in the lemon juice. Add the coconut milk mixture and stir well. Arrange the tomatoes, carrot, onion, and cucumber around the ahi, and sprinkle everything with 1 teaspoon pepper and scallions and sesame seeds, if using. Serve immediately, tossing the tuna and vegetables together at the table.

MEAT & POULTRY

PAN-SEARED STEAK

WITH GREEN HERB SAUCE

■ **SERVES 4 TO 6** As much as I love grilling steaks outdoors, sometimes I don't feel like dealing with stoking the fire. It may be pouring rain or too cold, or I'm simply being lazy. On those days, pan-searing steak is the way to go. Take the few extra minutes to season the meat ahead of time—ideally the night before—because it makes a huge difference in the results. The green herb sauce is fresh, savory, and a fantastic accompaniment. Don't shy away from it because of the anchovies! You won't taste anything fishy—rather, they melt away, leaving a salty umami flavor that you'll want to slather all over your steak. You may even want to double the green herb sauce recipe—it's that good.

I know many people don't like to flip their steaks more than once, but for this particular method, I find that flipping often allows a crust to develop more evenly and thickly, while the inside continues to cook steadily. I wait for 3 minutes before the first flip to ensure that the meat has released from the pan.

2 New York strip steaks, 1½ to 2 inches thick (2 pounds total)

Kosher salt and freshly ground black pepper

2 large garlic cloves

4 oil-packed anchovy fillets

2 tablespoons finely chopped fresh parsley

2 tablespoons finely chopped fresh basil

¼ teaspoon crushed red pepper flakes

6 tablespoons extra-virgin olive oil

1 tablespoon grapeseed oil or other high-heat neutral oil (see page 20)

1. Place a wire rack over a rimmed baking sheet. Heavily season both sides of the steaks with salt and black pepper. Place the steaks on the wire rack and refrigerate them, uncovered, for at least 8 hours or up to overnight. About an hour before you plan on eating the steaks, remove them from the refrigerator and bring them to room temperature.

2. Using a mortar and pestle (or a small food processor), mash the garlic, anchovies, parsley, basil, red pepper flakes, and ¼ teaspoon salt into a paste. It should take a few minutes of pounding to create a well-incorporated paste. Whisk in the olive oil until combined. Taste and season with more salt as desired.

3. If there is any moisture on the surface of the steaks, pat them dry with paper towels. Heat a large cast-iron skillet over high heat. Add the grapeseed oil. When the oil starts to shimmer, add the steaks and cook for 3 minutes on the first side. Flip the steaks over and cook, turning them often, until a dark golden brown crust has formed on each side and the internal temperature reaches 120°F for medium-rare, 130°F for medium, or your desired doneness.

4. Transfer the steaks to a cutting board and tent them loosely with aluminum foil. Let them rest for 10 minutes before slicing the meat against the grain. Serve with the green herb sauce slathered over the steaks.

DRY-BRINING MEATS

When I have time for it, I love to dry-brine steak, chicken, or pork before cooking it. This simple technique involves salting the meat and letting it sit in the refrigerator for at least 8 hours or as long as overnight. That time allows the meat to first expel liquid before reabsorbing it—and taking the salt with it. The salt then seasons the meat inside while also helping it retain moisture during cooking. And the surface of the meat dries out, which means you can get an excellent crust on it. Perfect!

Pan-Seared Steak with
Green Herb Sauce

BISON SHEPHERD'S PIE

1 pound Yukon Gold potatoes, peeled and cut into 2-inch cubes

1 pound rutabaga, peeled and cut into ½-inch cubes

½ cup half-and-half

4 tablespoons unsalted butter

Kosher salt and freshly ground black pepper

1 tablespoon grapeseed oil or other high-heat neutral oil (see page 20)

1 pound ground bison

1 large onion, chopped

1 large carrot, peeled and chopped

1 tablespoon all-purpose flour

1 tablespoon tomato paste

1 cup dry red wine

1 cup chicken stock, homemade (see page 68) or store-bought

1 teaspoon Worcestershire sauce

4 to 6 ounces kale (about ½ bunch), ribs removed, leaves sliced into ribbons

1 cup fresh or frozen peas

1 tablespoon finely chopped fresh parsley

1 tablespoon finely chopped fresh thyme

1 teaspoon finely chopped fresh rosemary

■ SERVES 6 TO 8 Shepherd's pie is the perfect hearty, cozy antidote for a cold, rainy day. Before I started cooking it myself I assumed that it was a daunting dish to make, but it is actually quite easy. Most of the ingredients are ones that I have on hand, except perhaps the rutabaga. I like to keep ground meats in my freezer for an occasion like this one—when I'm craving comfort food and want a satisfying one-dish meal without too much work. I like to use bison here because it's lower in saturated fat than lamb, while still packed with protein and flavor.

You can pack this shepherd's pie with more vegetables if you are trying to clean out your fridge and/or sneak in some extra nutrition. Mushrooms, parsnips, or more greens would all be lovely. Traditionally the mash that tops the pie involves only potatoes, but I like to put some rutabaga in there, both for flavor and for added nutrient variety. All in all, this shepherd's pie is healthier than most, and every bit as delicious.

1. Put the potatoes and rutabaga in a large pot and add cold water to cover by at least 2 inches. Bring to a boil over high heat, then reduce the heat to medium-low. Simmer until the root vegetables are fork-tender, about 25 minutes.

2. Meanwhile, in a small saucepan, warm the half-and-half and butter together over medium-low heat. Once the butter has melted, remove the pan from the heat and whisk in 1¼ teaspoons salt and 1 teaspoon pepper. Keep warm.

3. Drain the root vegetables in a colander and return them to the empty pot. Cook over low heat until all the excess water has evaporated, about 1 minute. Remove the pot from the heat and, using a potato masher or a ricer, mash the vegetables. Stir in the heated half-and-half mixture. Taste and season with more salt and pepper as desired.

••• recipe continues •••

4. Preheat the oven to 375°F.

5. In a large skillet set over medium-high heat, heat the grapeseed oil. Add the bison and cook, using a wooden spoon to break up the meat, until it has browned, about 8 minutes. Add the onion, carrot, ½ teaspoon salt, and ½ teaspoon pepper and cook until the vegetables have softened and are beginning to color, about 5 minutes. Add the flour and stir to combine. Cook, stirring, for 1 minute. Add the tomato paste and stir to combine. Cook, stirring, until the paste takes on a rust color, about 2 minutes. Add the wine and stock and stir, scraping up any browned bits on the bottom of the skillet. Cook until most of the liquid has cooked off, about 5 minutes. Remove the skillet from the heat and stir in the Worcestershire, kale, peas, parsley, thyme, and rosemary. Taste and season with salt and pepper as desired.

6. Spread the bison mixture evenly in the bottom of a 9 x 13-inch baking dish. Dollop the root vegetable mash on top and use a rubber spatula to spread it evenly over the bison mixture, making sure to cover it completely. Bake until the topping is golden brown, 30 to 35 minutes. Let the shepherd's pie cool for 5 to 10 minutes before serving.

PORK SCHNITZEL

WITH RED CABBAGE APPLE SLAW

SCHNITZEL

4 boneless top loin pork chops, each ½ inch thick

½ cup all-purpose flour

2 large eggs

1 tablespoon whole-grain mustard

1½ cups panko bread crumbs

1 tablespoon mustard powder

Kosher salt and freshly ground black pepper

6 tablespoons olive oil, for frying

SLAW

2 cups celery leaves (from about 2 bunches)

½ small head red cabbage, shredded (about 3 cups)

1 large carrot, peeled and cut into matchsticks

1 Granny Smith apple, peeled and cut into matchsticks

3 tablespoons extra-virgin olive oil

3 tablespoons apple cider vinegar

1 tablespoon honey

Kosher salt and freshly ground black pepper

■ SERVES 4 When I was growing up, both of my parents worked full-time. Consequently, they had arranged for my sister and me to be watched by an older couple during the day. We called them our babysitters, but they were more like another set of grandparents. Henny was from Germany and cooked all sorts of hearty German fare, from sauerbraten to goulash to *lebkuchen*. This recipe is my homage to her. Instead of serving the schnitzel alongside the traditional braised red cabbage, I lightened it up with a side of fresh, crunchy slaw.

1. **Prepare the schnitzel** Put a large piece of plastic wrap on a work surface, arrange the pork loin chops in a single layer on the plastic wrap, and top them with a second sheet of plastic wrap. Using a mallet or a rolling pin, pound the chops until they are an even ¼ inch thick. Don't be afraid to be forceful with this. Pork can be a bit tough, so feel free to take out any aggressions on the cutlets!

2. Set up three shallow pans for dredging. Place the flour in one pan. Whisk the eggs and whole-grain mustard together and pour the mixture into the second pan. Combine the bread crumbs, mustard powder, 1 teaspoon salt, and 1 teaspoon pepper in the third. Dip each cutlet in the flour, then the egg mixture, then the bread crumb mixture, shaking off any excess between dips. Place the breaded cutlets on a rimmed baking sheet and refrigerate it, uncovered. (Although not necessary, refrigerating the cutlets allows the breading to firm up and adhere to the meat better during frying. You can bread the chops several hours before cooking.)

3. **Make the slaw** In a large bowl, toss together the celery leaves, red cabbage, carrot, and apple.

•••• recipe continues ••••

1 tablespoon unsalted butter

1 large shallot, finely chopped
(about 4 tablespoons)

1 tablespoon all-purpose flour

½ cup dry white wine

½ cup chicken stock, homemade
(see page 68) or store-bought

2 tablespoons whole-
grain Dijon mustard

1 tablespoon heavy cream

Freshly ground black pepper

Kosher salt

4. In a small jar, combine the extra-virgin olive oil, vinegar, honey, ½ teaspoon salt, and ¼ teaspoon pepper. Seal the jar and shake it vigorously to combine. Pour the vinaigrette over the cabbage mixture and toss well. Taste and season with more salt and pepper as desired. (If breading the chops ahead of time, feel free to make the slaw ahead as well.)

5. Preheat the oven to 200°F. Set a wire rack on a baking sheet and place several layers of paper towels on top of the rack.

6. Heat a large cast-iron sauté pan over medium-high heat. When the pan is hot, add 3 tablespoons of the olive oil and 2 of the cutlets (give the cutlets room in the pan). Cook until the breading is golden and the cutlets are cooked through, 2 to 3 minutes per side. Transfer the cutlets to the paper towels and season each one with a pinch of salt. Wipe out any excess oil in the pan. Add the remaining 3 tablespoons olive oil and repeat with the remaining 2 cutlets. Put the cutlets in the oven to keep warm while you prepare the mustard sauce.

7. **Make the mustard sauce** Wipe any excess bread crumbs out of the sauté pan and reduce the heat to medium-low. Add the butter. Once the butter has melted, add the shallot and cook, stirring, until it is soft and translucent, about 5 minutes. Raise the heat to medium. While whisking with one hand, sprinkle in the flour with the other. Cook, whisking, for 1 minute to cook off the raw flour taste. Then whisk in the white wine and cook until the bubbling subsides, 1 minute. Whisk in the chicken stock and mustard, and cook until the liquid has reduced by half, about 5 minutes. Remove the pan from the heat and whisk in the cream and ½ teaspoon pepper. Taste and season with salt as desired.

8. To serve, spoon the mustard sauce onto the center of each serving plate. Place a cutlet on top of the sauce and pile the slaw on top of the cutlets. Serve immediately.

DRAINING AFTER FRYING   After sautéing or frying, it is extremely important to drain off any excess fat in order to achieve the crispiest crust. The best way to do this is the combination of paper towels over a cooling rack. The paper towels wick away excess fat and the rack allows air to circulate.

PORK TENDERLOIN

WITH PICKLED PLUM SAUCE

■ SERVES 4   I have family on Kauai, and we would visit them every summer when I was a kid. Even though Kauai is a small island, driving anywhere can take a while because there are no freeways. If we were going to spend some time driving, my mom or auntie would give us these salted dried plums called *li hing mui* to enjoy in the car (to help ease motion sickness). They can be quite an acquired taste, but I love their combination of sweet, sour, and salty. This plum sauce was inspired by my love of *li hing mui,* though the taste is much more approachable.

If you have the time, season the tenderloin the night before and let it rest in the fridge, which essentially dry-brines the pork (see sidebar on page 165).

1 tablespoon light brown sugar

Kosher salt and freshly ground black pepper

1½ pounds pork tenderloin, fat and silverskin removed

1 or 2 whole cloves

1 teaspoon whole Sichuan peppercorns

⅛ teaspoon fennel seeds

½ star anise pod

⅛ teaspoon ground cinnamon

2 cups chopped pitted fresh plums (1-inch cubes; about 6 plums)

1 (1½-inch) piece fresh ginger, unpeeled, sliced into coins (about the thickness of a nickel)

¼ cup rice vinegar

1½ teaspoons granulated sugar

1 tablespoon grapeseed oil or other high-heat neutral oil (see page 20)

1. In a small bowl, whisk together the brown sugar, 1½ teaspoon salt, and ½ teaspoon pepper. Rub the mixture evenly over the pork tenderloin. Set it aside.

2. Place a large cast-iron skillet or other ovenproof sauté pan in the oven and preheat the oven to 450°F.

3. In a dry skillet, toast the cloves, Sichuan peppercorns, and fennel seed together over medium-low heat until fragrant, about 3 minutes. Transfer the spices to a mortar and pestle, and grind until you have a fine powder. (Alternatively, grind them in a spice grinder.) Combine the spice powder with the star anise and cinnamon.

4. In a small saucepan, combine the spice mixture, ¼ cup water, 1½ cups of the plums, the ginger coins, vinegar, granulated sugar, and 1 teaspoon salt. Cook over medium-low heat, stirring occasionally, until the plums have fully broken down, about 30 minutes. Remove and discard the star anise and ginger coins. Transfer the mixture to a blender and blend until smooth, 20 to 30 seconds. Return the mixture to the saucepan and set it aside while you cook the pork.

5. Carefully remove the hot cast-iron skillet from the oven and add the grapeseed oil. Place the pork tenderloin in the skillet, return the skillet to the oven, and roast until

the meat is browned on the bottom, 10 minutes. Carefully remove the skillet from the oven and flip the tenderloin over. Return the skillet to the oven and reduce the oven temperature to 375°F. Roast until the pork is cooked through and registers 140° to 145°F on an instant-read thermometer, 10 to 15 minutes. Transfer the pork to a cutting board, tent it loosely with aluminum foil, and let it rest for at least 5 minutes.

6. Meanwhile, place the plum sauce over medium-low heat. Add the remaining ½ cup chopped plums and cook until they are heated through, 5 minutes. Remove the pan from the heat. Taste the sauce and season with salt and pepper as desired.

7. Slice the pork into medallions and serve them with the plum sauce on the side.

PLUM SAUCE   You can make the plum sauce up to 3 days in advance. After pureeing the sauce in the blender, refrigerate it in an airtight container. When you are ready to enjoy the sauce, gently heat it in a saucepan over medium-low heat. Add the remaining ½ cup plums and let them heat through.

SOUS VIDE   The instructions here involve roasting the pork. This method produces a wonderfully moist, tender pork tenderloin, though another method that you can use is sous vide, if you have the equipment and prefer to cook the pork this way. Simply sous vide to 145°F, and then quickly sear the sides of the tenderloin in a cast-iron skillet before serving it.

Pork Tenderloin with
Pickled Plum Sauce

CHICKEN ADOBO

■ SERVES 6 TO 8 If there is one dish that defines my childhood, this is it. My mom would make chicken adobo on a weekly basis, and nothing calls up memories of those years like the scent of simmering vinegar and soy sauce. Mom would break down a whole chicken into its parts for this recipe, and I would always reach for the drumstick. Now, when I make it for myself, I use *only* drumsticks, but you can use any chicken cuts you prefer. Just make sure to use bone-in pieces to add flavor. Therein lie the best qualities of adobo: it's extremely forgiving and you can change it up to fit your preferences. The basic ratio is 2:1, vinegar to soy sauce, and while Filipino cane vinegar is more traditional, I prefer the fruitiness of apple cider vinegar. Honestly, you can use white vinegar, rice vinegar, red vinegar . . . they all make a great adobo!

I like to serve this with roasted broccoli and steamed rice to sop up the delicious sauce. Enjoy!

10 skin-on chicken drumsticks

1⅓ cups apple cider vinegar

⅔ cup soy sauce or tamari

⅔ cup chicken stock, homemade (see page 68) or store-bought

2 tablespoons light brown sugar

8 garlic cloves, thinly sliced

3 bay leaves

Freshly ground black pepper

1½ tablespoons cornstarch

¼ cup coconut cream (optional; see Note)

3 scallions, light green parts only, thinly sliced, for garnish

1. Arrange an oven rack 5 to 6 inches from the heating element and preheat the broiler to high.

2. In a medium to large saucepan, nestle the drumsticks in one layer. Add the vinegar, soy sauce, chicken stock, brown sugar, garlic, bay leaves, and 2 teaspoons pepper. Bring to a boil over high heat, then reduce the heat to medium-low. You want the mixture to cook just slightly above a simmer. Partially cover the pan and cook, turning the drumsticks every 5 minutes or so, until the chicken is barely cooked through, about 20 minutes. Transfer the chicken to a plate and pat it dry with paper towels.

3. Remove and discard the bay leaves. Cook the vinegar mixture over medium-low heat until it has reduced and thickened, about 5 minutes. Ladle about ½ cup of the mixture into a small bowl and whisk in the cornstarch until it has dissolved. Whisk the cornstarch mixture into the vinegar mixture in the saucepan and cook until the sauce has thickened to a gravy-like consistency, about 1 minute. Remove the pan from the heat and whisk in the coconut cream (if using). Keep the sauce warm while you finish the chicken.

4. Place the dried drumsticks on a baking sheet and broil until the skin is crisp and dark golden brown in places, 3 to 5 minutes.

5. Remove the drumsticks from the broiler and arrange them on a platter. Sprinkle with the scallions and serve the warm adobo sauce on the side.

COCONUT CREAM   I like to add a little coconut cream at the end of the cooking to mellow out the vinegar punch, but you can skip it if you want. My mom and grandma never added it, though my great-grandma did. To get the cream from a can of full-fat coconut milk, do not shake the can before opening it. Scoop out the solid cream and reserve the remaining milk for something else, such as a Mango Coconut Smoothie (page 202). The cream will be easier to extract if the can is a bit cool, so refrigerate it for about 30 minutes before opening.

CHICKEN STOCK   Save the bones for making chicken stock! Just pick off any parts that have the adobo sauce on them and throw the bones in a plastic zip-top bag to store in the freezer.

MAKE AHEAD   If you would like to prepare the chicken ahead of time, combine the chicken with the vinegar, soy sauce, chicken stock, brown sugar, garlic, bay leaves, and pepper in a large plastic zip-top bag and let it marinate in the fridge for a few hours. This step is optional and one that I often skip, but it will allow the flavor to permeate the chicken a bit more. It's an easy way to get a jump on your day. Just dump the contents in the saucepan when you're ready to cook!

Chicken Adobo

SLOW COOKER COQ AU VIN

4 bone-in, skin-on chicken legs

Kosher salt and freshly
ground black pepper

6 ounces thick-cut bacon
(2 or 3 slices), chopped

1 large onion, coarsely
chopped (about 2 cups)

2 medium carrots, peeled
and coarsely chopped
(about 1½ cups)

1 small garlic clove, thinly sliced

12 ounces button mushrooms,
stemmed and quartered

2 cups dry red wine, preferably
Pinot Noir or Burgundy

1 cup chicken stock, preferably
homemade (see page 68)

10 sprigs fresh thyme

1 sprig fresh rosemary

1 bay leaf (fresh or dried)

Roasted potatoes or buttered
egg noodles, for serving

Finely chopped fresh
parsley leaves, for garnish

■ SERVES 4 TO 6   Slow cookers are great for a number of reasons, but my favorite is that you can clean up the kitchen while the meal cooks away. Enjoying my dinner without a pile of dirty dishes waiting for me at the end really helps me wind down. Plus, I can set the slow cooker before I leave the house in the morning and come home to a perfectly cooked coq au vin.

This dish takes a bit of preparation, but it's worth it. In order to get perfectly cooked chicken skin and those browned bits that add a ton of flavor, you need to start the chicken in a Dutch oven. If you simply added raw chicken to the slow cooker, the final dish would suffer. I like to prepare everything the night before and let the browned chicken and vegetables marinate in the fridge overnight. Blending the vegetables at the end of the recipe may seem like an unnecessary step, but it makes for the most luscious sauce. The texture of the vegetables is long gone after the extended cooking time, and this gives them a delicious second life.

1. Using a sharp chef's knife, separate the chicken thighs from the drumsticks (or have your butcher do this for you). Season the pieces with salt and pepper.

2. Heat a large Dutch oven over medium-low heat. Add the bacon and cook, stirring occasionally, until it is crisp, 10 to 12 minutes. Resist the temptation to turn up the heat; patience is key when rendering bacon. Using a slotted spoon, transfer the bacon to an airtight container, leaving the rendered fat in the pan, and refrigerate it until serving time.

3. Raise the heat to medium-high. Working in batches, add the chicken pieces to the rendered fat and cook until the skin is a deep golden brown on all sides, about 30 minutes total. Transfer the chicken to a plate.

4. Reserving 1 tablespoon, pour the fat from the Dutch oven into a heatproof jar and set it aside. With the Dutch oven still over medium-high heat, add the onion and carrots

to the reserved fat and cook, stirring occasionally and scraping up any browned bits with a wooden spoon, until the vegetables are soft, about 3 minutes. Add the garlic and cook, stirring, until fragrant, about 1 minute. Spread the vegetables out in the bottom of a slow cooker.

5. Reduce the heat under the Dutch oven to medium-low. Add 1 tablespoon of the reserved fat and add the mushrooms. Cook, stirring, until they are browned, about 10 minutes. The mushrooms will first soak up all the fat, but after a few minutes, they'll release liquid. If they start to burn, add more fat. Season them with a pinch of salt and cook until all the liquid has evaporated, about 1 minute. Transfer the mushrooms to an airtight container and refrigerate until serving time.

6. Pour 1 cup of the wine into the Dutch oven and cook, scraping up any browned bits on the bottom of the pot. This may take some time, but there is a lot of flavor in those bits! It's worth the elbow grease. When all the browned bits are incorporated into the wine, remove the pot from the heat.

7. Place the chicken, skin-side up, on top of the vegetables in the slow cooker. Pour the wine sauce over the chicken, and add the remaining 1 cup wine and the chicken stock. Using butcher's twine, tie the thyme, rosemary, and bay leaf into a bundle, and nestle the herbs among the chicken. Cover the slow cooker. (At this point, you can refrigerate the chicken for as long as overnight to let it marinate in the wine.)

8. Cook on Low in the slow cooker for 4 hours (or up to 6 hours if needed). When the chicken is cooked through, transfer it to a platter. Discard the herb bundle. Place the vegetables and any liquid in a high-powered blender and blend until smooth. Pour the sauce back into the slow cooker, return the chicken to the cooker, and add the reserved mushrooms and bacon. Cover and cook on Low until heated through, 10 minutes.

9. Serve the coq au vin over roasted potatoes or buttered egg noodles, garnished with parsley.

DON'T HAVE A SLOW COOKER? NOT TO WORRY!

Set a rack in the middle of the oven and preheat the oven to 350°F. After you have cooked the bacon, browned your chicken, sautéed your vegetables, and deglazed the pan, simply continue cooking the coq au vin in the Dutch oven: Spread the vegetable mixture in the deglazed pot, adding it to the wine. Arrange the browned chicken, skin-side up, in a single layer. Add the remaining wine and the stock. Nestle the herb bouquet in the center. At this point, you can set the entire mixture aside to marinate in the fridge up to overnight, or you can place it in the oven right away to finish cooking. (If you allowed the mixture to marinate in the fridge, heat the Dutch oven, uncovered, on the stovetop over medium heat. Once the mixture begins to simmer and the oven has reached 350°F, place a lid on the Dutch oven and transfer it to the oven.)

Bake the coq au vin for 1 hour, until the chicken is cooked through and tender. Discard the herb bundle and transfer the chicken to a platter. Place the vegetables and any liquid in a high-powered blender and blend until smooth. Pour the sauce back into the Dutch oven, and add the chicken and the reserved mushrooms and bacon. Warm over low heat until heated through, about 10 minutes, and serve.

ROASTED CHICKEN LEGS

WITH KABOCHA SQUASH

■ **SERVES 4** I find roasted chicken to be one of the most comforting meals. This particular recipe is the perfect versatile one-pot dish for chilly winter nights, and it requires very little work to put it together. I love kabocha squash here, but feel free to try other hearty vegetables; root vegetables (carrots, rutabagas, turnips, sweet potatoes) and winter squash work particularly well, but almost any vegetable—whole mushrooms, fennel, onion—will do nicely. Sometimes I even thinly slice Meyer lemons, skin and all, and throw those in with the other veggies. They are not necessary by any means, but they will add a citrusy note to the final dish.

I like to serve this family-style, straight out of the cast-iron pan. All you need is a mixed green salad and a side of whole grains, such as steamed farro or wheat berries, to round out this hearty meal. As you dig in, squeeze the soft roasted garlic out of its papery skin and spread it onto the meat and veggies.

4 bone-in, skin-on chicken legs (drumsticks and thighs attached)

Kosher salt and freshly ground black pepper

4 tablespoons olive oil

1 small kabocha squash, peeled, seeded, and cut into 1½-inch cubes (see Note, page 186)

1 head of garlic, separated into cloves (papery skin left on)

½ bunch fresh thyme sprigs

1. Place a rack in the center of the oven and preheat the oven to 375°F.

2. Heat a large cast-iron skillet or other large ovenproof pan over medium-high heat. Season the chicken with salt and pepper. Add 2 tablespoons of the olive oil to the pan, followed by the chicken, skin-side down. Do not crowd the pan, so work in batches if necessary. Cook the chicken until the skin is golden brown, about 10 minutes. Turn the chicken over and cook the second side until browned, 4 to 6 minutes. Transfer the chicken to a plate and remove the pan from the heat. Discard any fat that has accumulated in the pan.

••• recipe continues •••

3. While the pan is still hot, add the squash, garlic, thyme, and remaining 2 tablespoons olive oil. Season with salt and pepper and toss well. Spread the mixture evenly in the pan and nestle the chicken legs on top of the veggies. Cover the pan with the lid or aluminum foil.

4. Roast the chicken and vegetables in the oven for 45 minutes. Then uncover the pan, raise the oven temperature to 400°F, and roast until the chicken skin is browned and crisp, about 15 minutes. Serve hot.

CHICKEN TIPS   If you have the time, and space in your fridge, dry-brine the chicken up to a day before you plan on cooking it (see the sidebar on page 165).

Even if you don't plan on eating the skin, leave it on for cooking—it adds a ton of flavor to the finished dish and ensures that the meat stays super moist.

Don't forget to save those chicken bones for homemade stock! After picking the meat off the bones, store the bones in a plastic zip-top bag in the freezer until you're ready to make a batch of stock (see page 68).

KABOCHA   Kabocha squash has very tough skin. For easier peeling, carefully cut off the top and bottom of the squash. Then, using either a paring knife or a vegetable peeler, peel the squash from top to bottom.

FILIPINO STREET NOODLES

1 (16-ounce) package thin rice stick noodles

1½ pounds lean pork, such as boneless top round, thinly sliced on an angle

Kosher salt

3 tablespoons peanut oil

2 cups thinly sliced onion

4 garlic cloves

3 medium carrots, peeled and cut into 1-inch matchsticks

8 ounces green beans, trimmed, strings removed if any, cut into 1-inch pieces

1 red or orange bell pepper, thinly sliced

4 celery stalks, thinly sliced on an angle

1 medium napa cabbage, shredded

1½ cups chicken stock, homemade (see page 68) or store-bought

½ cup soy sauce or tamari, plus more for serving (optional)

Freshly ground black pepper

1 pound shrimp (40/60 count), peeled and deveined, cut in half lengthwise

1 tablespoon Kitchen Bouquet or liquid Maggi seasoning (see Note, page 129)

Calamansi (see Note, page 188) or lemon wedges, for garnish

Fish sauce, for serving (optional)

■ SERVES 10 TO 12   *Pancit bihon* is basically the Filipino answer to Chinese street noodles. After my grandma's lumpia (page 128), her *pancit* is my next favorite dish, and it's served at every family gathering. I can remember a handful of Thanksgivings where I skipped the traditional American fare altogether and ate only lumpia and *pancit!* This dish started my lifelong addiction to any and all noodle dishes, especially the Asian variety. This recipe makes a very large amount, which is perfect for feeding a group, and it keeps well, too, though for only a couple of days.

1. In a medium bowl, cover the noodles with cold tap water. Let them soak until softened, 10 minutes. Drain and set aside.

2. Heat a very large, deep saucepan, wok, or Dutch oven over medium-high heat. Add the pork, ½ cup water, and a pinch of salt. Bring to a boil, then reduce the heat to medium-low. Simmer until the pork is no longer pink, about 6 minutes. Drain the pork in a colander set over a bowl, reserving the cooking liquid.

3. Return the pan to medium-high heat and add 1 tablespoon of the peanut oil. Add the pork and cook, stirring, until it is very lightly browned, about 4 minutes. Transfer the pork to a plate. Add the onion and garlic to the pan and cook, stirring, until they are beginning to soften, 2 minutes. Add the carrots, green beans, and bell pepper and cook, stirring, until they are beginning to soften, 4 minutes. Add the celery, cabbage, ½ cup of the chicken stock, ¼ cup of the soy sauce, ½ teaspoon salt, and ⅛ teaspoon black pepper. Toss until the vegetables are coated in the liquid, then push them to one side of the pan. Add the shrimp to the other

•••• recipe continues ••••

side of the pan and cook, stirring, just until they turn pink, about 3 minutes. Add the pork and stir the whole mixture to combine. Transfer it to a large bowl.

4. In the same pan set over medium-high heat, heat the remaining 2 tablespoons peanut oil. Add the softened rice noodles, reserved pork cooking liquid, remaining 1 cup chicken stock, remaining ¼ cup soy sauce, and 1 tablespoon of the Kitchen Bouquet. Cook, stirring well, until the noodles have soaked up all the liquid, 6 to 8 minutes. Add two-thirds of the vegetable, pork, and shrimp mixture to the noodles and stir well until heated thoroughly. Transfer the mixture to a large serving bowl. Top with the remaining vegetable, pork, and shrimp mixture.

5. Serve family-style, with the calamansi wedges on the side and either fish sauce or soy sauce for each person to add to taste.

FILIPINO LIMES   Calamansi is a small Filipino citrus that's similar to a sour lime. The entire fruit is edible, like a kumquat. The flesh is very sour, but the skin has a mild sweetness. You may be able to find them at a farmer's market or an Asian grocery store. If you can't, not to worry. You can substitute lemon wedges.

COMFORT RAGU

2 large onions, cut into quarters

4 celery stalks, coarsely chopped

3 large carrots, peeled
and coarsely chopped

6 garlic cloves

6 fresh sage leaves

1 pound ground beef (80% lean)

1 pound ground pork

1 pound ground veal (see Note)

Kosher salt and freshly
ground black pepper

2 tablespoons olive oil

1 tablespoon all-purpose flour

1 (750 ml) bottle dry red wine

1 (28-ounce) can
crushed tomatoes

Freshly grated nutmeg

1½ teaspoons ground cinnamon

½ cup half-and-half

Cooked fresh pappardelle or
pasta of your choice, for serving

Grated Parmesan
cheese, for serving

Chopped fresh parsley,
for serving

■ MAKES 4 QUARTS (EACH QUART SERVES ABOUT 4 OVER PASTA)

Essentially my version of Bolognese sauce, this recipe is, hands down, the dish my friends and family request the most. Its stick-to-your-ribs quality is ideal for our cold, rainy winter nights in Northern California. This recipe creates a big batch because it freezes beautifully, too, which makes it my favorite gift to give new moms or anyone who would benefit from a little comfort food.

Serve this sauce tossed with fresh pappardelle pasta and showered with grated Parmesan and chopped fresh parsley. Though I know that fresh parsley is not a traditional garnish for Bolognese sauce (per my Italian fans on Instagram!), I love the brightness and added nutrition that it gives the final dish. You can also use this sauce as the base for *lasagna alla bolognese*.

1. Using a food processor, pulse the onions, celery, carrots, garlic, and sage together until the mixture is relatively homogenous with some texture remaining.

2. Heat a large Dutch oven over medium-high heat. Season the ground meats with salt and pepper. Add 1 tablespoon of the olive oil to the Dutch oven. Working in batches (so that you don't steam the meat), add the ground meats and cook, using a wooden spoon to break up the meat, until it browns, 20 to 25 minutes total. Remove the meat with a slotted spoon and set it aside. There will be quite a bit of rendered fat from the meats, but don't be alarmed. You will be able to remove the excess fat at the end of the recipe, but leave it in the pot at this point.

3. Add the remaining 1 tablespoon olive oil (for more flavor) and the chopped vegetables to the pot. Season with a generous pinch of salt. Cook, scraping up any browned bits that are stuck on the bottom of the pot, until the excess moisture from the vegetables is cooked off, about 15 minutes. Return the cooked meat to the pot and stir well. Sprinkle the flour over the mixture and stir well. Cook, stirring occasionally, for 2 minutes. Add the wine and crushed tomatoes. Sprinkle a pinch of nutmeg over the

mixture and add the cinnamon. Season with a pinch of salt and a generous amount of pepper. Bring the sauce to a boil, then reduce the heat to medium-low. Simmer, uncovered, stirring occasionally, for 2 hours. Add the half-and-half and cook, stirring occasionally, for 1 more hour.

4. There will likely be a good amount of fat that has risen to the top of the sauce by the end of the cooking time. Using a ladle, remove most of this excess fat and discard it. Leave just a little bit of the risen fat and stir it back into the sauce. Taste and season the sauce with more nutmeg, salt, and pepper as desired.

5. To serve, divide the pappardelle among serving bowls, ladle the ragu over the pasta, and sprinkle generously with Parmesan and parsley. Any leftover sauce will keep in an airtight container in the refrigerator for 5 days or in the freezer for up to 6 months.

HUMANELY RAISED VEAL   While it is possible to get humanely raised veal in the United States, I completely understand if you would prefer not to eat it. If that is the case, feel free to substitute 1 pound ground beef chuck.

SMOOTHIES, JUICES & SWEETS

EVERYDAY GREEN SMOOTHIE

8 to 10 ounces kale (about 1 large
bunch), coarsely chopped

4 ounces collard greens (about
½ bunch), coarsely chopped

3 or 4 celery stalks,
coarsely chopped

½ cup coarsely chopped
fresh parsley leaves

16 ounces frozen pineapple

1 large banana, very ripe

1 Granny Smith apple, cored
and cut into wedges (optional)

⅓ cup fresh lime juice
(from about 2 limes)

¼ cup fresh lemon juice
(from about 1 lemon)

¼ teaspoon Maldon
sea salt (optional)

■ MAKES 4 SMOOTHIES Green smoothies are part of my daily diet, and I often enjoy them as my afternoon snack. If your goal is to be your healthiest self, incorporate them into your routine. Nutrition experts differ on many ideas, but they universally agree that Americans need to eat more fruits and vegetables, especially leafy greens. Smoothies are the easiest way to consume a large amount of fruits and vegetables in a portable, easily digestible form. One can eat only so many salads!

Depending on what's in season, you can change up the ingredients, but a few remain constant in my smoothies. Dark leafy greens are the base; romaine, chard, spinach, or any leafy green can easily substitute for the kale or collards. Citrus, particularly limes and lemons, are high in vitamin C, which helps you absorb the iron in the greens. The high acidity in the citrus also cuts through the bitterness of the greens. If you want to counteract the bitter green flavors even more, try adding a Granny Smith apple. This is also an ideal electrolyte drink—while many people drink electrolyte replacement drinks when they're active, they're often filled with many unnecessary (or even harmful) ingredients, such as high-fructose corn syrup. The salt is optional, but as an electrolyte, it adds to the hydration benefit (I opt for sea salt for the additional minerals, too).

I use the entire leaf and stem of the kale and collard greens since my Vitamix takes care of the tougher fibrous parts, but if you don't have a high-powered blender, simply remove and discard the stems first.

1. In a high-powered blender, working in two or three batches, blend the kale and collard greens with 2 cups water until the mixture is uniform and smooth, 30 to 45 seconds. If you have a tamper on your blender, using it will help break down the greens. Turn off the blender, add the celery and parsley, and blend until smooth, 30 to 45 seconds. Add the pineapple, banana, apple (if using), lime and lemon juices, and salt (if using) and blend until smooth. Top off the mixture with enough water to make 64 ounces total. Blend for another few seconds to fully incorporate.

2. Divide the smoothie among four 16-ounce mason jars, seal tightly, and store in the fridge for up to 3 days, or enjoy immediately. The smoothie may separate a bit if stored in the fridge; just shake the jar before enjoying it.

BANANAS   I always like to have very ripe—almost too ripe—bananas on hand for smoothies. I buy a bunch and intentionally let it ripen on the counter to this stage. Then I peel all the bananas, cut them in half, transfer them to a large zip-top plastic bag, and store them in the freezer.

CHERRY-ALMOND RECOVERY SMOOTHIE

■ MAKES 1 SMOOTHIE Recovery nutrition—which involves consuming some calories, protein, and fat within thirty minutes of an intense workout—is incredibly important during training, as it helps replenish the body's energy stores and repair muscles. Smoothies are the easiest, most portable way to get some good nutrition immediately after a workout.

This smoothie quickly became my favorite post-workout drink because it is delicious and packed with essential nutrients to aid the body's recovery. Cherries have natural anti-inflammatory properties, which can help ease the wear and tear of intense training; whole-milk Greek yogurt has a great tangy, creamy taste and adds necessary fat and protein; and the chia seeds contribute protein along with omega-3 fatty acids. Sounds pretty stacked!

1 cup unsweetened almond milk, preferably homemade (see page 207)

1 cup frozen pitted dark cherries

½ frozen very ripe banana (see Note, page 195)

½ cup full-fat Greek yogurt (see Note)

2 tablespoons chia seeds

In a blender, combine the almond milk, cherries, banana, and yogurt and blend until the mixture is uniformly smooth. Add the chia seeds and process until they are thoroughly incorporated. Enjoy within several hours.

GREEK YOGURT If you are watching your total calories, feel free to substitute 2% fat Greek yogurt. Keep in mind that a little bit of fat helps recovery, so I would avoid the nonfat variety.

SMOOTHIE-TO-GO To bring this smoothie to your workout, pack it into a double-walled, insulated stainless steel water bottle. I like to pour some ice water into the water bottle first and allow it to chill the inside of the bottle for 5 minutes or so, then dump the water out and pour in the prepared smoothie. This way you can bring your smoothie to your workout even if you don't have a refrigerator. The chia seeds will thicken the smoothie as it sits, but it will otherwise keep for several hours.

WATERMELON SLUSHIE

■ MAKES FOUR 16-OUNCE SLUSHIES Staying hydrated is important for everyone, but it's especially important for an athlete. Due to the nature of our sport, swimmers have to stay on top of hydration more than most. Since we're in the water, we're never aware of how much water we're losing— and trust me, we lose a lot! Plain water is so boring that I can tolerate only so much. I like to stay hydrated with fruit- or herb-infused water, an Everyday Green Smoothie (page 194), herbal tea, or with the food that I consume.

Watermelon is the perfect food for hydration. It's mostly water, yet it's packed with vitamins, amino acids, and antioxidants. It's a great source of vitamins A, B_6, and C, as well as the antioxidant lycopene, while still being low in calories. Among the many benefits of lycopene, this powerful antioxidant helps fight inflammation in the body—another plus.

This slushie is incredibly refreshing after a tough workout or simply as a summertime treat. The lime juice balances the sweetness of the watermelon and gives a boost of vitamin C. The sea salt also plays off the watermelon's sweetness while adding to the hydration benefits.

1 (8- to 9-pound) seedless watermelon (see Note)

⅓ cup fresh lime juice (from about 2 limes)

¼ teaspoon Maldon sea salt

4 tablespoons packed fresh mint (optional)

1. Cut the watermelon in half, then cut each half lengthwise into quarters. Cut the flesh out of the watermelon rind. Working in batches, process the watermelon flesh in a blender until it is liquefied, pouring the juice into a large pitcher or container as you go. Add the lime juice and salt, and stir until fully incorporated.

2. Pour roughly half the juice into ice cube trays and freeze them for 8 hours or overnight. Store the remaining juice in the refrigerator (it will keep for up to 3 days).

3. To make one 16-ounce slushie, blend 8 ounces watermelon juice, 8 frozen cubes of watermelon juice (each ice cube is about 1 ounce), and 1 tablespoon mint (if using).

RIPE WATERMELONS To find a ripe watermelon, choose one that seems heavy for its size. Gently rap a knuckle on the melon; a ripe one will sound hollow.

FROZEN WATERMELON MARGARITAS This slushie makes a delicious margarita, too! Just add blanco tequila to taste.

STRAWBERRY OAT SMOOTHIE

■ MAKES 2 SMOOTHIES This smoothie should be added to your morning or pre-workout routine for many reasons beyond the fact that it is simple and delicious. It's full of protein and probiotics from the kefir, insoluble fiber from the oats to keep you full and energized for hours, and prebiotics from the bananas. Kefir is a great source of probiotics, which have been shown to aid in digestion, promote good gut health, and positively affect the immune system. The prebiotics in the bananas are a type of fiber that feed the probiotics in your gut, thus keeping them healthy.

2 cups plain kefir (see Note)

2 cups frozen strawberries

½ cup old-fashioned rolled oats

2 tablespoons ground flaxseed

1 very ripe fresh or frozen banana

2 teaspoons honey (optional)

In a blender, combine the kefir and strawberries and blend on high speed until the strawberries are fully pureed and blended. If the mixture is having a hard time getting started, add a splash of water. Add the oats, flaxseed, and banana. Blend on high speed until the oats are fully blended into the smoothie, about 30 seconds. Taste the smoothie and if it needs more sweetness, add the honey. Blend briefly to combine and serve.

KEFIR I like the tartness of the plain kefir, but if it's too tart for you, substitute vanilla-flavored kefir.

MANGO COCONUT SMOOTHIE

■ MAKES 1 SMOOTHIE   I love adding fresh herbs to smoothies because they are filled with aromatic oils and packed with antioxidants. Anyone who grows mint knows that it can quickly take over a garden. This smoothie is a good way to use up some of that refreshing mint while throwing in some added nutrition with the spinach. A tropical drink with a healthy twist, this drink is a perfect snack for that time of day when you have a craving for something a little sweet.

1 cup full-fat unsweetened coconut milk

1 cup frozen mango

1 cup firmly packed baby spinach

½ cup fresh mint leaves

½ frozen very ripe banana (see Note, page 195)

In a high-powered blender, combine the coconut milk, mango, spinach, mint, and banana. Blend until uniformly smooth and to your desired consistency. Enjoy right away, or store the smoothie in an airtight container in the refrigerator for up to 3 days.

PERFORMANCE BEET JUICE

■ MAKES TWO 10-OUNCE JUICES Beets are a wonderful superfood with numerous health benefits, including aiding athletic performance. Raw beets are a good source of dietary nitrates, which get converted to nitric oxide by beneficial bacteria in our mouths and saliva. Nitric oxide has been shown to increase a body's tolerance for high-intensity exercise and allows our muscles to work more efficiently. Additionally, beets and ginger are both filled with antioxidants that help fight inflammation. Beet juice is best drunk as a pre-workout or pre-race beverage and should be enjoyed with a small meal, because raw beets can upset an empty stomach. While I love the taste of beets, some people can find them to be too earthy—the fresh lemon juice here brightens the flavors.

1 (17.5-ounce) can coconut water

¼ cup fresh lemon juice (from about 1 large lemon)

2 medium beets (about 8 ounces), trimmed, peeled, and cut into quarters

2 teaspoons grated fresh ginger

1. In a high-powered blender, combine the coconut water, lemon juice, beets, and ginger. Blend until well combined, about 30 seconds. Keep in mind that the beets are raw, so to ensure they're liquefied, you can let the blender go longer than you think is necessary.

2. Using a fine-mesh sieve, strain the mixture, pressing on any solids with a rubber spatula. Discard the solids. Enjoy immediately or store the juice in an airtight container in the refrigerator for up to 3 days.

CANTALOUPE JUICE

WITH BLACK PEPPER SYRUP

■ SERVES 4 TO 6   This *agua fresca*–like drink is a very popular summertime beverage in the Philippines. The traditional version is super simple—essentially shredded cantaloupe, water, and sugar—but so refreshing. My grandma would make this drink for my cousins and me during the hottest days of summer, when melons are at their peak, using her special melon-scraper tool. This juice is also great fully blended, and I actually prefer it that way.

I switched up the basic recipe a bit to make it more interesting and to take out the excess sugar. The grated turmeric adds a healthy dose of antioxidants and enhances the beautiful orange color of the melon. Black pepper may seem like an odd ingredient, but trust me on this! It elevates the juice's flavor and also helps you absorb the antioxidants in the turmeric. This juice is best served as cold as possible.

1 large cantaloupe

1½ tablespoons grated fresh turmeric

Kosher salt

Black Pepper Syrup (recipe follows), to taste

Fresh mint sprigs, for garnish

1. Place a fine-mesh strainer over a large pitcher or other container. Cut the melon in half and scrape the seeds into the strainer. Press on the seeds with the back of a spoon to get as much juice and flesh off the seeds as you can. Discard the seeds.

2. Cut each melon half lengthwise into 4 pieces, then cut the rind off each slice. Coarsely chop the melon and add it to a blender along with the strained juice/flesh and 2 cups water. Turn the blender on high speed and blend thoroughly. Stir in the turmeric and a generous pinch of salt. Top off the mixture with water until the total volume is 8 cups (it'll probably be a lot of water) and blend again. Refrigerate for at least 4 hours or up to overnight.

••• recipe continues •••

3. To serve, pour the juice over ice. Stir in black pepper syrup to taste. Garnish each glass with a fresh mint sprig.

CANTALOUPE When choosing a cantaloupe, find one that seems heavy for its size. The rind should smell fragrant and sweet and the rind should have an orange color. Rinds that have a lot of green or white are underripe. Gently press on the top of the melon, where the vine was attached; it should be slightly soft.

TRADITIONAL TECHNIQUE

If you want to go the traditional route with extra texture, simply grate the cantaloupe, top it off with enough water to total 8 cups, and then proceed with the recipe. Assuming that you don't own a melon scraper (I know I don't), just use the largest grating blade of your food processor. I've seen people use a fork to hand-grate the melon, but a food processor is so much easier. Do not forget to stir the mixture before serving and divide the cantaloupe pulp among the serving glasses.

BLACK PEPPER SYRUP

■ MAKES ABOUT 2 CUPS This spicy yet floral syrup is surprisingly lovely when added to cantaloupe juice. Use high-quality Tellicherry peppercorns for the most flavorful syrup. Keep any leftovers to use in cocktails.

2 cups water

1 cup sugar

Freshly ground black pepper

In a small saucepan set over high heat, combine the water, sugar, and 1½ tablespoons pepper. Whisk until the sugar has completely dissolved. Reduce the heat to medium-low and gently boil the mixture until it has reduced to a syrupy consistency, 20 minutes. Strain the syrup through a cheesecloth-lined fine-mesh sieve into a container; discard the pepper. The strained syrup will keep in an airtight container in the refrigerator for a few months.

SPICED ALMOND MILK

■ MAKES ABOUT 1½ QUARTS   I generally use almond milk for my smoothies (as in the Cherry-Almond Recovery Smoothie on page 197) and rarely drink the milk straight, but this is an exception. The blend of warm spices in creamy milk is reminiscent of eggnog, so I make this a lot during the holidays to quell any cravings.

The unfortunately named nut milk bag can be purchased at quality or natural grocery stores or at health food stores. They cost a couple dollars and make such a difference in the overall texture of the milk. A few layers of cheesecloth can be used if you can't find a nut milk bag, but the almond milk will not be as silky.

Enjoy this almond milk warm or cold. To make plain almond milk, follow this recipe, adding the dates and salt but omitting the cinnamon, vanilla, cardamom, and nutmeg. Shelf-stable almond milks are filled with preservatives, sweeteners, and/or stabilizers. Freshly made almond milk tastes much better than anything you can buy in the store. I never liked almond milk until I started making my own!

2½ cups natural whole (raw) almonds

2 or 3 pitted Medjool dates

¼ teaspoon Maldon sea salt

1 teaspoon vanilla paste or extract (see Note, page 39)

1½ teaspoons ground cinnamon

½ teaspoon freshly ground cardamom (from 3 to 5 green cardamom pods)

½ teaspoon freshly grated nutmeg

1. Place the almonds in a large bowl or container and add water to cover by several inches. Put the bowl in the refrigerator and let the almonds soak for at least 8 hours and up to 48 hours.

2. Drain the almonds in a colander and transfer them to a high-powered blender. Add water to make a total of 8 cups. Blend on high speed for about 30 seconds or until the mixture resembles an almond milk.

3. With one hand, hold a nut milk bag open over a large bowl while you use the other hand to pour the almond mixture into the bag. Once you have all of the mixture in the bag, close the drawstring and start squeezing! Continue squeezing until there is no more liquid in the nut milk bag. This process should take a few minutes. Discard the almond pulp left in the bag and return the strained almond milk to the blender.

•••• recipe continues ••••

4. Add the dates and salt, and blend on high speed for about 30 seconds or until the dates are well incorporated. Add the vanilla, cinnamon, cardamom, and nutmeg. Blend for a few seconds until incorporated, then transfer the milk to a large mason jar or divide it among a few jars and seal the lid(s). The blender will make the almond milk very foamy, but the foam will go down.

5. The milk will keep in the refrigerator for 3 to 5 days. The spices will separate from the almond milk as it settles in the fridge, so just shake the jar a bit before enjoying it. You can enjoy this milk cold or warm. If you prefer it heated up, simply warm it in a small saucepan over medium-low heat.

SPICED ALMOND PUDDING

I sometimes use this recipe to make a nutrient-dense dessert packed with omega-3 fatty acids, protein, and fiber. Simply combine ¼ cup chia seeds with 1 cup of the Spiced Almond Milk. Whisk every 5 minutes or until the chia seeds are suspended in the milk, which takes 15 to 20 minutes. Refrigerate overnight for the mixture to become thick like a pudding. Enjoy!

FILIPINO STICKY COCONUT RICE

■ MAKES ABOUT 24 SQUARES My grandma makes many different versions of this dessert-style sticky rice with coconut, called *bibingkang malagkit* (pronounced: "bee-bing-kah mah-lug-kit"), but this one, with a hint of anise, is my favorite. It's a wonderful dessert to make ahead of time because it keeps well and is delicious at room temperature. *Masarap* (which means "delicious" in Tagalog)!

2 cups sweet rice (also known as glutinous rice)

1 tablespoon coconut oil

2 (13.5-ounce) cans full-fat unsweetened coconut milk, unopened

1½ cups packed light brown sugar

Kosher salt

1 teaspoon pure anise extract

2 cups finely shredded unsweetened coconut

1. Put the rice in a sieve, set the sieve inside a large bowl, fill the bowl with water, and stir the rice with your hands. The water will become cloudy. Lift the sieve out of the water to drain the rice; discard the water. Repeat until the water remains clear. Then fill the bowl with water one more time and let the rice soak in the sieve for at least 1 hour and up to 12 hours. (This technique allows the rice to cook more evenly.)

2. Preheat the oven to 350°F. Grease a 9 x 9-inch baking dish with the coconut oil, then line it with parchment paper, leaving a couple of inches of overhang (this will make it easier to lift the dessert out of the baking dish).

3. Shake the cans of coconut milk before opening them, then pour the milk into a large liquid measuring cup. Add water until you have a total of 4 cups. Pour the liquid into a medium saucepan. Drain the rice well, add it to the liquid, and set the pan over high heat. Bring to a boil, stirring often to prevent the rice from sticking to the bottom of the pan, then reduce the heat to low. Cover the pan and cook, stirring occasionally, until the rice is tender and has absorbed most of the liquid, 20 to 30 minutes.

••• recipe continues •••

4. Remove the pan from the heat. Stir in the brown sugar, ¼ teaspoon salt, and anise extract. The mixture should be thick and chewy. Transfer the rice mixture to the prepared baking dish. Using your hands or a rubber spatula, flatten the mixture evenly in the dish.

5. Put the dish in the oven and bake for 20 minutes. Then raise the oven temperature to 375°F and bake until the top of the *bibingkang* is golden brown and bubbling, another 20 minutes. Remove the pan from the oven and let the dish cool completely.

6. Reduce the oven temperature to 350°F. Spread the shredded coconut evenly over a rimmed baking sheet and toast it until lightly golden, about 5 minutes. Remove the baking sheet from the oven and immediately transfer the coconut to a bowl so it doesn't continue to toast on the pan. Sprinkle one-third of the coconut on top of the *bibinkang*.

7. Transfer the *bibingkang* to the refrigerator to firm up for at least 2 hours. It will be easier to cut it when it is chilled.

8. Lift the *bibingkang* out of the baking dish and invert it onto a cutting board. Peel off and discard the parchment paper, and sprinkle the top with half the remaining shredded coconut. Cut it into 24 squares. Roll the sides of the squares in the remaining toasted coconut. If making ahead, the *bibingkang* will keep in an airtight container in the refrigerator for 3 to 5 days. Serve at room temperature.

HALO HALO

1 tablespoon jarred or canned azuki beans (also called "yude azuki")

1 jarred whole palm seed (usually labeled "palm seed whole in syrup"), chopped

2 tablespoons jarred *macapuno* strings (also called "coconut sport")

1 teaspoon jarred purple yam jam (also called "ube halaya")

1 piece canned jackfruit in syrup, drained and very thinly sliced

Shaved ice (see Note)

1 teaspoon sweetened condensed milk, or more to taste

1 scoop *ube* or *macapuno* ice cream (optional)

⅓ cup evaporated milk

■ SERVES 1   I'm generally someone who prefers salt to sweet, so I rarely crave desserts—but this dish is a major exception. *Halo halo* means "mix mix" in Tagalog and involves a wonderful combination of sugary (often canned) fruit topped with shaved ice and evaporated milk. On a hot summer day, there is nothing like it!

Traditional *halo halo* is often topped with anything from ice cream and toasted cereal to candies to tapioca pearls—you name it! This recipe uses my favorite combination of toppings, and while I won't scoff at ice cream on my *halo halo*—particularly *macapuno-* or *ube*-flavored ice cream—it's not necessary. When my grandma would make this for all the grandkids, she never included ice cream. It wasn't until I started seeing *halo halo* at shaved ice stands in Hawaii that I realized it usually has it. It's not the healthiest dessert, so I'm sure she was just trying to limit the excess.

From the *ube* (Filipino purple yam) ice cream to the whole palm seed, you will likely have to visit an Asian market to get many of these ingredients. The canned fruits and beans will come in all sorts of can sizes, so just buy the size that you think you will use. *Macapuno* is sometimes labeled "coconut sport" or "mutant coconut." Despite the name, it is a naturally occurring variant of the coconut where the endosperm develops abnormally, resulting in jelly-like, sweet coconut flesh.

1. In a large glass, layer in the azuki beans, palm seed, *macapuno*, purple yam jam, and jackfruit. Fill the glass with enough shaved ice to reach the top. Drizzle the condensed milk over the shaved ice. Top with a scoop of ice cream (if using). Pour the evaporated milk over the top, allowing it to drip down through the shaved ice.

2. To enjoy the "mix mix," stir the ingredients together with a long spoon. The perfect bite has a little bit of everything mixed together.

SHAVE ICE WITH A FOOD PROCESSOR   A shaved ice machine is the superior tool for making shaved ice, but you can make an ice "snow" using your food processor or blender. Fill a food processor halfway with ice cubes. Pulse until the mixture resembles fine snow, 15 to 20 pulses. If using a blender, turn the blender on high speed before adding the ice. Add the ice one handful at a time while shielding the top of the blender with the other hand. Continue doing this until you don't hear any more ice bouncing in the blender. While a regular blender will do, a high-powered one like a Vitamix is best.

DESSERT LUMPIA

■ MAKES 6 LUMPIA; SERVES 6 Known as *turon,* dessert lumpia calls for only a few ingredients. Saba bananas are much smaller and starchier than the bananas we usually see in stores. You should be able to find saba bananas at an Asian market, but if you can't, substitute ripe plantains; you'll need to cut them to a smaller size, since the lumpia are usually 4 inches long. Traditionally *turon* are very sweet, as they're made with lots of brown sugar, but I prefer to tone down the sweetness. Feel free to add more brown sugar if you like. Frying in oil is the traditional method for preparing these treats, but I have provided an oven-fried version if you prefer.

3 pieces canned jackfruit in syrup, drained

6 lumpia wrappers

3 ripe saba bananas, cut in half lengthwise

¼ cup firmly packed dark brown sugar

1 egg white

Vegetable oil, for frying

1. Set a wire rack over a baking sheet and place several layers of paper towels on the rack.

2. Dry the jackfruit pieces well with paper towels. Unroll the jackfruit and slice each piece crosswise into 6 pieces.

3. Keep the lumpia wrappers covered with a clean damp dish towel or paper towels while you are assembling each lumpia. Lay a wrapper in front of you on your work surface, so it forms a diamond shape. Place 1 banana slice in the center, with the ends of the banana pointing toward the left and right corners of the wrap. Sprinkle 1 to 2 teaspoons of the brown sugar evenly over the banana. Place 3 slices of jackfruit over the banana slice. Brush the top edges of the wrapper with some of the egg white. Fold the bottom corner over the banana, then fold the left and right corners in toward the center and over the fruit. Tightly roll the lumpia up, sealing the edges. It should be about 4 inches long and 1½ inches in diameter. Repeat with the remaining wrappers and fillings.

4. When you are ready to cook the lumpia, brush them all over with the remaining egg white. Heat 3 inches of vegetable oil in a medium pot set over high heat. When the oil reaches 375°F, put 2 lumpia into the hot oil. The oil should bubble vigorously. Cook the lumpia until they are golden brown all over, about 2 minutes per side. Using a spider or a slotted spoon, transfer the lumpia to the paper towel–lined rack to drain. Repeat with the remaining lumpia. Serve hot.

OVEN-FRIED LUMPIA

Alternatively, you can oven-fry the lumpia. Preheat the oven to 425°F. Line a baking sheet with parchment paper and spray the parchment with cooking spray. Arrange the lumpia on the baking sheet with a few inches of space between them. Heavily spray the lumpia with cooking spray and bake until they are golden brown all over, 20 to 25 minutes. The wrapper won't get as crispy as the deep-fried version, but it will still be tasty.

ACKNOWLEDGMENTS

There are so many people that I would like to thank.

First and foremost, I want to thank my mom. Despite working full-time and often commuting, you always managed to cook delicious dinners for Megan, Dad, and me. We always had our favorites: chicken adobo, chiles rellenos, or corned beef, cabbage, and rice. (I never knew that white rice wasn't the traditional side dish for corned beef!) I was a picky eater when I was younger, and I'm sure that was tough. Now, thanks to you, I have a love for fancy mixed greens, even though for the longest time Megan and I called them "weeds" and turned up our noses at anything but romaine. You often made traditionally unhealthy fare much better for us, and we never noticed a difference. And you have always appreciated tradition and celebrating with food; my favorite dish you concocted for such purposes is either your "Marco Polos" for Christmas Day or the *halo halo* birthday cake you made for me.

••• continued •••

Thank you to Grandma Bohn. I'm so grateful that you kept such meticulous records of Great-Grandma Aguillon's recipes and shared them with me. Thank you for always making a mountain of lumpia for family gatherings. No one's lumpia, my own included, will ever compare to yours. I will never forget our massive Thanksgiving dinners with both traditional Filipino and American fare, and the many times I spoiled my appetite with your lumpia—it was always totally worth it. Thank you for making *halo halo* and cantaloupe juice for my cousins and me on hot summer days. And thank you for helping me write all the Filipino recipes in this book and answering my many questions.

Thank you to my loving husband, Ethan, for always being an eager taste tester. I still have no idea how one person can eat so much and stay so fit. Your love of food matches my own, and I truly enjoy pursuing it with you. Thank you for giving great feedback throughout the process of writing this book, making many trips to the grocery store with me, and helping me clean the huge messes I made in the kitchen. You've always loved my cooking, even when I was just starting out and had a lot to learn. We've shared so many memorable meals throughout the years, ranging from a twenty-two-course tasting menu at the Restaurant at Meadowood on our anniversary to campfire-cooked trout while camping in Arnold. Each and every meal has a special place in my heart.

Thank you to my sister, Megan, for giving me so many great ideas throughout the writing process and for testing some of my recipes. We may not have gotten along so well growing up, but I couldn't be more thankful that you are my sister!

Thank you to my dad for being wonderfully supportive. You showed me what it means to work hard and have determination. You and Mom recognized how competitive I was at an early age and helped me funnel that energy toward the pool. I'm so grateful for your constancy and encouragement throughout my life, but especially during my athletic career. And you always loved and championed me the same way, whether I won an Olympic gold medal or I was disqualified.

Thank you to Grandpa Bohn, a most amazing grandpa. I will never forget the many times I heard your booming voice call out "Go Bears!" during the silence before the start of a race. It meant a great deal to me to know you were there supporting me, along with the rest of my crew: Ethan, Mom, Dad, Megan, Grandma, and Tom. I have been so lucky to have you guys follow me all around the world. And no one will ever carve the prime rib on Christmas Eve the way you do.

Thank you to Tom, my unofficial godfather. You have traveled the world to see me swim more than anyone else and have always been my very own travel consultant whenever I was in a new country or stuck in a new airport. Thank you for always giving me my special Belgian chocolates before my most important competitions. They gave me that extra edge!

Thank you to Henny and Danny Stanchina for taking such great care of Megan and me while our parents were at work. You both cooked such great food for us and taught us how to appreciate the garden. Henny, I blame my love affair with a genuine frankfurter on you, as well as my love of coffee. Danny, thank you for being a surrogate grandpa and for making my favorite egg pasta whenever I asked. And I will never forget the many times that you walked with me to get a chocolate-dipped vanilla Fosters Freeze as a treat. Thank you for having always been so kind, patient, and loving with Megan and me.

Thank you to Alicia Kendig at the United States Olympic Committee for answering my many nutrition questions throughout the years. I love your approach to nutrition and the way you always give real-world, attainable advice. You have helped me and countless other athletes make the most of this very important piece of the athletic puzzle. The United States Swim Team is so lucky to have you.

Thank you to my longtime agent, Janey Miller, for being such a great friend for so many years and for helping me throughout my professional career. You've always been so much more than an agent to me. Thank you for helping me make this cookbook a reality and for giving me the push that I needed to start the process.

Thank you to my literary agent, Farley Chase, for recognizing my passion for food and cooking, and for putting me in touch with the right people. Without you, this book would have never happened.

Thank you to the many people at Clarkson Potter who contributed their talents and expertise to the making of this book. It's beautiful! Thank you especially to my editor Jennifer Sit, designer Sonia Persad, production editor Cathy Hennessy, production manager Kevin Garcia, publicist Jana Branson, and Stephanie Davis in marketing. Thank you also to the talented photo team, including photographer Erin Kunkel, food stylist Abby Stolfo, prop stylist Claire Mack, and Devon Lach.

And, finally, thank you to Ashley Meyer for helping me edit this book. I always wanted to write a cookbook, and you helped me achieve that lifelong goal. I knew that I had a voice but I feared that it would be lost in the process, so I'm very thankful that you helped make my recipes and stories come to life. Thank you, also, for testing so many of my recipes and searching for hard-to-find ingredients when they were out of season. Thank you for holding my hand throughout this daunting process and making it so much easier for me. I would have been a stress case without you.

Last but not least, thank you to all the friends, family, and coaches who have supported me throughout my life. I have been so very fortunate to have so many great people in my life. I love you all!

INDEX

Note: Page references in *italics* indicate photographs.